ALSO BY GERALD G. MAY

The Awakened Heart

Addiction and Grace

Care of Mind, Care of Spirit

Will and Spirit

Pilgrimage Home

Simply Sane

The Open Way

THE DARK NIGHT OF THE SOUL

THE

DARK NIGHT

OF THE

SOUL

A Psychiatrist Explores the
Connection Between Darkness
and Spiritual Growth

GERALD G. MAY, M.D.

HarperSanFrancisco
A Division of HarperCollins*Publishers*

For Sr. Constance FitzGerald, O.C.D.,

and Fr. John Welch, O.Carm.,

whose teaching unlocked for me the treasures of

John of the Cross and Teresa of Ávila

HarperCollins books may be purchased for educational, business, or sales promotional use. For information please write: Special Markets Department, HarperCollins Publishers, Inc., 10 East 53rd Street, New York, NY 10022.

HarperCollins Web site: http://www.harpercollins.com

HarperCollins®, 📖®, and HarperSanFrancisco™ are trademarks of HarperCollins Publishers, Inc.

FIRST EDITION

Library of Congress Cataloging-in-Publication Data

May, Gerald G.

    The dark night of the soul : a psychiatrist explores the connection between darkness and spiritual growth / Gerald G. May. — 1st ed.

      p. cm.

    Includes bibliographical references.

    ISBN 0–06–055423–1 (cloth)

      1. Mysticism—Psychology. 2. Spiritual formation—Psychology. 3. Teresa, of Avila, Saint, 1515–1582. 4. John of the Cross, Saint, 1542–1591. 5. Suffering—Religious aspects—Christianity. I. Title.

BV5083.M32   2003

248.2—dc22   2003056966

Designed by Ralph L. Fowler

04 05 06 07 08 ❖RRD(H) 10 9 8 7 6 5 4 3 2 1

CONTENTS

Contents

ACKNOWLEDGMENTS

M any thanks go to Constance FitzGerald and
John Welch, to whom this book is dedicated.
They introduced me to the wisdom of John and
Teresa, and much of my work is based on their understandings. The conclusions and interpretations in
this text are mine, however, and I bear full responsibility for any distortions I may have included. There
are a good many other Carmelites to whom I am
indebted, including Kieran Kavanaugh and Otilio
Rodriguez, for their excellent translations of John's
and Teresa's work; Tessa Bielecki, for her Teresan

anthologies; Barbara Jean LaRochester, who remembers my birthday; and Kevin Culligan, who always sends me a card on the feast day of St. Gerald of Mayo.

I am deeply grateful for the ongoing encouragement of my colleagues at the Shalem Institute (www.shalem.org) and especially to my wife, Betty, for her continual love and support as well as her indispensable help with Spanish translation.

Most of the English translations included herein are my own versions, based on standard Spanish compilations and—since I am not fluent in Spanish myself—relying heavily on E. A. Peers's classical editions as well as the Kavanaugh and Rodriguez translations and the assistance of other, more able Spanish speakers. I have tried in all cases to render the meanings in a way appropriate to the discussion. I have indicated in the notes where I have directly quoted material from the Institute of Carmelite Studies translations, and appreciate their permission to do so.

INTRODUCTION

Our responding to life's unfairness with
sympathy . . . may be the surest proof of
all of God's reality.

—*Rabbi Harold Kushner*[1]

Wmen people speak of going through a dark
night of the soul, they usually mean they're
experiencing bad things. The bad news is that bad
things happen to everyone, and they have nothing to
do with whether you are a good or bad person, how
effectively you've taken charge of your life, or how
carefully you've planned for the future. The good
news, or at least part of it, is that good things happen
to everyone too.

At the outset I must confess that I am no longer
very good at telling the difference between good
things and bad things. Of course there are many
events in human history that can only be labeled as

evil, but from the standpoint of inner individual experience the distinction has become blurred for me. Some things start out looking great but wind up terribly, while other things seem bad in the beginning but turn out to be blessings in disguise. I was diagnosed with cancer in 1995, which I thought was a bad thing. But the experience brought me closer to God and to my loved ones than I'd ever been, and that was wonderfully good. The chemotherapy felt awful, but it resulted in a complete cure, which I decided was good. I later found out it may also have caused the heart disease that now has me waiting for a heart transplant. At some point I gave up trying to decide what's ultimately good or bad. I truly do not know.

Although not knowing may itself seem like a bad thing, I am convinced it is one of the great gifts of the dark night of the soul. To be immersed in mystery can be very distressing at first, but over time I have found immense relief in it. It takes the pressure off. I no longer have to worry myself to death about what I did right or wrong to cause a good or a bad experience—because there really is no way of knowing. I don't have to look for spiritual lessons in every trouble that comes along. There have been many spiritual lessons to be sure, but they've been *given* to me in the course of life; I haven't had to figure out a single one.

One of the biggest lessons—and another gift of the dark night—is the realization that I'm not as much in control of life as I'd like to be. This is not an easy learning, especially for take-charge people like me, people who think they can—and, more important, *should*—be in control of things. Other people are more naturally able to go with the flow of life. They deal with things as best they can and then go on to the next moment. They too have their dark nights, times of confusion and seeming powerlessness, but they don't pester themselves. Either way, each experience of the dark night gives its gifts, leaving us freer than we were before, more available, more responsive, and more grateful. Like not knowing and lack of control, freedom and gratitude are abiding characteristics of the dark night. But they don't arrive until the darkness passes. They come with the dawn.

In 1981, when Harold Kushner published his tender classic *When Bad Things Happen to Good People*, few people outside monastic walls had heard of the dark night of the soul. Those who did know of it generally felt it was an elite mystical phenomenon—something reserved for the holiest saints. But times change, and now the "dark night of the soul" has become a catch phrase in the circles of pop spirituality, where it is used to describe all kinds of misfortunes from major life tragedies to minor disappointments.

In part, I am writing this book because I'm convinced that both of these understandings, the old and the new, are wrong. The dark night of the soul is not restricted to holy people. It can happen to anyone. I believe that in some ways it happens to everyone. Yet it is much more significant than simple misfortune. It is a deep transformation, a movement toward indescribable freedom and joy. And in truth it doesn't always have to be unpleasant!

If you have never heard of the dark night of the soul, I hope this book will give you an appreciation of what it means historically and, more important, what it might mean in your own life. The dark night is a profoundly good thing. It is an ongoing spiritual process in which we are liberated from attachments and compulsions and empowered to live and love more freely. Sometimes this letting go of old ways is painful, occasionally even devastating. But this is not why the night is called "dark." The darkness of the night implies nothing sinister, only that the liberation takes place in hidden ways, beneath our knowledge and understanding. It happens mysteriously, in secret, and beyond our conscious control. For that reason it can be disturbing or even scary, but in the end it always works to our benefit.

More than anything, I think the dark night of the soul gives *meaning* to life. It is a meaning given in not knowing, as Dag Hammarskjöld tried to describe in one of his final writings:

> *I don't know Who—or what—put the question. I don't know when it was put. I don't even remember answering. But at some moment I did answer Yes to Someone—or Something—and from that hour I was certain that existence is meaningful and that, therefore, my life, in self-surrender, had a goal.*[2]

The meaning revealed in the dark night is beyond understanding. As with Hammarskjöld, one cannot fully comprehend it. But one is left with an ever deepening certainty that the meaning is there, that life is much more than coping and adjustment. Mysterious as it may be, there is something wonderful at the heart of our existence, and it is about nothing other than love: love for God, love for one another, love for creation, love for life itself.

During the twenty-five years I practiced medicine and psychiatry, I had the honor of accompanying many people in their struggles to cope with suffering. Often we were able to discover ways of easing the pain. Sometimes, we even found a sense of meaning in it. All too often though, our preoccupation with finding relief left little opportunity to look for meaning. This is the curse of a health-care system dedicated only to fixing problems, a system too streamlined to be concerned with what's happening to people's souls.

Frustrated, I found myself gradually leaving the practice of medicine and dedicating myself more to the art of spiritual companionship. Here the priorities are reversed; we continue to care about easing suffering, but the meaning is what's most important. It was in this context that I first encountered St. John of the Cross's writings about the dark night of the soul.

It was strange that I should have been so taken
with his insights. My Methodist parents had left me
with a healthy suspicion of all things Catholic—
especially saints. Even my Catholic friends got sour
looks on their faces at the mention of John of the
Cross. They called him austere, harsh, even life-
denying. But I was reading his poetry and there was
nothing harsh about it, no austerity at all, nothing
even saintly. The poems I was reading were songs of
soaring passion, full of love, sensual yearning, and
delight. And there wasn't a single religious word in
them.

¡Oh noche que guiaste!	Oh you guiding night!
¡Oh noche amable más	Oh night more kindly
que el alborada!	than the dawn!
¡Oh noche que juntaste	Oh you night that united
Amado con amada,	Lover with beloved,
amada en el Amado	the beloved in the Lover
transformada!	transformed![3]

I can't avoid sounding like a New Age fanatic as I
speak of this, but the more I read, the more it seemed
this sixteenth-century Spanish friar understood me—

actually knew me at the deepest level of my being. More than Freud or Jung or any of the other psychiatric authorities I'd read, John described my own experience. Further, he made sense of it.

For reasons that will become clearer as we proceed, John of the Cross has been seriously misinterpreted and misunderstood. The dark night of the soul, in John's original sense, is in no way sinister or negative. It is, instead, a deeply encouraging vision of the joys and pains we all experience in life. It inspires the desire to minimize suffering and injustice wherever possible, and at the same time it sheds a hope-filled light on the pains that cannot be avoided. It is too wonderful a thing to remain esoteric and too profound to be trivialized.

Another misunderstanding—the one that finally prompted me to write this book—is the assumption that authentic spiritual growth requires great and dramatic tragedy. It's a myth that takes many forms, from "Suffering is good for the soul" to "No pain, no gain." It has even been used to justify human suffering as somehow being "God's will."

Many people have confided in me that they feel their spiritual lives are somehow deficient because

they have not suffered enough. Certainly life brings
suffering; no one escapes it. But John of the Cross's
insights have helped me understand that suffering
does not result from some divine purgation designed
for a spiritual elite. Instead, suffering arises from the
simple circumstances of life itself. Sometimes human
suffering is dramatic and horrifying. More often it is
ordinary, humble, and quiet. But neither way is it
"God's will." The divine presence doesn't intend
us to suffer, but is instead *with* us in all the experiences of life, in both suffering and joy. And that
presence is always inviting us toward greater freedom
and love.

A related misunderstanding is that the dark night is
something that occurs once in a lifetime, that one gets
through it and moves on to some permanent state of
realized union and spiritual ecstasy. John himself may
be partly responsible for this confusion; some of his
commentary is very linear indeed. His own life, however, tells a different story. So does John's most important mentor and spiritual guide, Teresa of Ávila.
Confessing that the longest time she'd ever experienced such a dramatic state of union was "about
half an hour," Teresa maintained that "no one is so

advanced in prayer that they do not often have to return to the beginning."[4] I am convinced that instead of being a once-and-for-all experience, the dark night of the soul appears in various ways throughout our lives, always mysterious and always hopeful.

In large part, then, I write this book as a way of clearing up confusions I feel have distorted and covered over some very important aspects of the spiritual life. To enable this clarification, I'll be going back to the original sources frequently, citing John's and Teresa's work, often in their Spanish language. There are several problems with this. First, although many of Teresa's original manuscripts have survived, almost none of John's has. Thus even the Spanish editions of John's work are taken from handwritten copies, many of which are known to contain inaccuracies. Further, I am not at all good in Spanish myself. However, with the help of those who are fluent, a variety of competent translations, and my own interpretation of the contexts, I believe I have been able to grasp much of the original meaning. I am sure that here and there I have also added some of my own distortions in the process—I only wish I knew what they were so I could label them as such! But at least I will be offering another careful vision of the work of Teresa and John—one that I hope honors the original and is illuminated by modern understanding.

Language and authenticity of sources are not the only difficulties. The concept of the dark night originated half a millennium ago in a culture and theological context foreign to mine. The essential material John and Teresa share is all about the depths and dynamics of the human psyche, yet it lacks the sophisticated psychological and neurological insights that modern science has given us. But that difficulty has proven to be an exciting, mutually enriching process for me, as I hope it will be for you. The dark night of the soul can illuminate our modern experience, but today's knowledge can also illuminate the dark night of the soul.

This process of mutual illumination will also clarify some other concepts that popularization has distorted—things such as prayer, meditation, contemplation, and the process of human spiritual growth. But it won't do any better than Rabbi Kushner did in providing an answer to why bad things happen to good people. At the end of his book, Kushner points out that "the word 'answer' can mean 'response' as well as 'explanation.'" He suggests that the more important question is not why the bad things happen, but how we will respond to them.[5]

Kushner says that God's role in human suffering is to stand with us, giving us courage and strength and empowering us to respond with compassion and forgiveness. I agree. I also feel that the dark night of the soul reveals an even deeper divine activity: a continually gracious, loving, and fundamentally *protective* guidance through all human experience— the good as well as the bad.

For Teresa and John, the dark night—indeed all of life—is nothing other than the story of a love affair: a romance between God and the human soul that liberates us to love one another. If you are firmly convinced there is no God, this story will be a romantic fantasy, one that has generated some exquisite poetry. At the other extreme, if you are firmly convinced about who or what God is, you may have trouble with both the story and its poetry. For Teresa and John, the Beloved is endless Mystery, always beyond our capacity to comprehend. Therefore, if we have a choice, it is best for all of us to hold both our beliefs and disbeliefs lightly. Listen to the truth of your own life experience in the light of Teresa's and John's stories. That is where we begin.

• Duruelo

• Medina del Campo

Salamanca •

Fontiveros •

• Segovia

• Madrid

Ávila •

• Toledo

CHAPTER ONE

HALF A FRIAR

The Story of Teresa and John

That Jews and Christians, together with Muslims,
can live in amity, respecting differences while honoring
commonalities—that this is no pipe dream—is proven
by the fact that, for centuries, they did just that.

—*James Carroll*[1]

J ews, Christians, and Muslims did indeed live in
harmony in a time and place that "some remember as a kind of paradise." It is known as the *convivencia,* the "living together." The time was between the
ninth and twelfth centuries, and the place was Spain.
As Carroll recounts it, it was a time when Muslims
opened the doors of their mosques for Christian

worship services and when Jews were schoolmasters for Christian children. This rich cross-fertilization of faiths and cultures produced famous universities and renowned thinkers, including the great Jewish philosopher Moses Maimonides, who chose to write not in Hebrew, but in Arabic.

Religious warfare originating outside Spain began to dismantle the *convivencia* in the twelfth century, but vestiges of its rich heritage lasted into the sixteenth century, the time of Teresa of Ávila and John of the Cross. In many ways, Teresa and John inherited the creative legacy of the *convivencia*.

John of the Cross will forever be credited for the idea of dark night of the soul, but the inspiration wasn't his alone. John acknowledged his indebtedness to a number of previous authors, including an obscure sixth-century mystic who wrote under the name of Dionysius and spoke of "a ray of darkness."[2] Of all those who influenced John's work, however, the most important was Teresa, the woman he called his spiritual mother. Though he seldom acknowledged her as a source, nearly all of John's imagery and most of his fundamental insights can be found in Teresa's earlier writings. Thus to appreciate the meaning of the dark night, we must start with Teresa of Ávila.

Teresa

I n the rugged central highlands of Spain, fifty miles west of Madrid, is the ancient walled city of Ávila. It lies on the Adaja River, in a valley between two great mountain ranges: the Sierra de Gredos to the south and the Sierra de Guadarrama to the east. Teresa was born there in the cold early spring of 1515.

It was the last year of the reign of King Ferdinand; Isabella had died a decade earlier, after establishing the Spanish Inquisition, putting a formal end to the *convivencia* by expelling all Jews from Spain, and sending Columbus to the New World. Balboa had just claimed the entire Pacific Ocean in the name of Spain, and treasure from the Americas was making Spain the wealthiest and most powerful empire in the world. Elsewhere, Leonardo da Vinci had just painted the *Mona Lisa* and Michelangelo had finished his sculpture of David. Copernicus was developing his claim that the planets revolve around the sun, and two years later Martin Luther would nail his theses to the church door in Wittenberg.

Teresa was born into a wealthy family of textile merchants. Her grandfather had been a *converso*, a Jew forced to convert to Christianity by the Inquisition. Her father saw to the education of his twelve children and made sure his daughters learned to read and write at home—there was no public education for women. Teresa was bright, spirited, adventurous, and, like many children of the time, fervently religious. At the age of seven, inspired by reading the lives of the saints, she and a brother tried to run away from home and become martyrs, "to go to the land of the Moors . . . and have them cut off our heads." They were apprehended at the edge of town by an uncle, who returned them to their worried mother. "Our greatest obstacle," Teresa later wrote, "was that we had parents."[3]

When Teresa was twelve, her mother died. Soon thereafter, her father noticed that Teresa's passions had shifted from spirituality to romance novels and, of course, to boys. Concerned about her future, he sent her to a convent school when she was sixteen. He never wanted her to become a nun and could not have foreseen that her passions would revert, as they soon did, to prayer and a growing call to religious life.

Because her father was strongly set against her becoming a nun, Teresa struggled mightily with the decision. Perhaps in part because of this conflict, she

fell ill. The illness, the first of many that were to
plague her the rest of her life, forced her to leave the
school. Her recovery took nearly two years, during
which her sense of call to religious life grew even
stronger. Finally at the age of twenty, she convinced
her father of her determination and became a
Carmelite novice.

Less than two years after her profession as a nun,
she again became ill, eventually suffering a paralysis
of her legs that kept her an invalid for three years.
Then, at the age of twenty-seven, while praying to
St. Joseph, she experienced what she felt was a mirac-
ulous recovery. In that same year, 1542, less than
thirty miles away in the small village of Fontiveros,
John of the Cross was born.

John

J ohn's father, like Teresa's, had come from
a wealthy family of textile merchants. But
the family disowned him when he married John's
mother, a poor weaver far beneath his social station.
Thus, unlike Teresa, John was born into poverty.
Worse, his father died shortly after John was born,

leaving John and his mother and two older brothers destitute. After one of his brothers died, possibly from malnutrition, his mother moved to Medina del Campo. There she was able to place John in a church orphanage school, where he could be fed and educated. He excelled academically and as a teenager worked in a hospital as an orderly.

We have no evidence that he ever considered any career other than the religious life. At the age of seventeen, he entered the nearby Jesuit school and again excelled. He had established an impeccable reputation by the time he moved into formal theological studies. The director of the hospital where he worked wanted John to come back as a chaplain, and his Jesuit educators wanted him to join their order. But John desired a more contemplative lifestyle, and in 1563 he joined the Carmelite novitiate in Medina del Campo.

A Dark Night for Teresa

At the same time, back in Ávila, Teresa was approaching fifty and was making the final revisions on her first book, her *Life*. Things had not gone well for her during the past two decades.

It had started pleasantly enough, with her unexpected healing from the illness everyone thought would kill her. Upon her recovery, she expressed great devotion to St. Joseph, to whom she attributed the miracle of her healing. With typical passionate excess, she encouraged her sisters to do likewise. Apparently they were not hesitant in giving her feedback, and she soon realized she had succumbed to considerable spiritual pride.

She then turned her passion against herself, becoming excessively scrupulous and painfully conscious of all her other failings. She developed such disgust with herself that she felt unworthy even to pray. She gave up the practice of prayer for nearly two years, a decision she regretted for the rest of her life. Throughout her later writings, she repeatedly counsels others never to make the same mistake. There is no reason, ever, she says, to give up the practice of prayer.

A spiritual director finally convinced her to begin praying again, but Teresa continued to be besieged by self-doubts, now about her experiences in prayer. Not only was she preoccupied with distractions; she also heard God speaking to her and before long began to see inner visions of Christ. Such dramatic experiences were highly suspect in the spirituality of her time, especially for a woman. The experiences seemed valid to her while she was in prayer, but afterward, reflecting on them with others, she was terrified they might be the work of the devil.

Her early spiritual directors confirmed her fears. They were certain the voices and visions came from the devil, and Teresa was sent from one counselor to another. One told her to abstain from quiet prayer and solitude. Obediently, she tried never to be alone. But her prayer was irrepressible. Even when she was with other people, "The Lord made me recollected during conversation and . . . would say what He pleased. . . . I had to listen." Another director even ordered her to make the "fig," a contemptuous hand gesture like today's "finger," at any vision of Christ she might experience. She obeyed, though "it was a horrible thing to do and caused me great pain."[4]

Liberation

These fears and self-doubts plagued Teresa for twenty years and did not cease until she was about forty-seven. In her *Life* she describes how the struggles came to a close. In the end, she surrendered—neither to her own judgments nor to those of her spiritual directors, but to God alone. She quit trying to control her prayer and instead simply put it in God's hands. Thereafter, she tested others' opinions against her own interior sense of authenticity in and with God.

She repeatedly affirms it was God's sheer grace that enabled her to surrender and to trust her own deepest perceptions. She describes three specific experiences, however, that were especially profound vehicles of that grace. The first two consisted of words she heard from God in prayer; the third came as validation by a single human being who finally understood her.

The words from God came at times when she was feeling especially disconsolate and abandoned. Once, after a trusted confessor had moved away and Teresa felt she was "bound to grow wicked again . . . as if my soul were in a desert," she heard God say, "I no longer want you to talk with men, but with angels." She took this to mean she only had to attend to counsel given by people she sensed were deeply in love with God. Another time, when she was feeling that "everyone was against me," she heard God say, "Do not be afraid, daughter, for I am here and will not abandon you." These experiences, she wrote, made her feel like a "new person" and gave her courage and fortitude. Nor did she doubt that the words came from God. "I would have argued with the whole world that this was God's work."[5]

The human validation came from a Franciscan friar whom Teresa met in Toledo in 1560. A man of deep prayer and devotion, Peter of Alcántara was widely respected for his asceticism. Teresa bared her soul to Peter, and "Nearly from the beginning, I could see that from his own experience he understood me. That was all I needed." The feeling was mutual. Peter so trusted Teresa's inner experience that he shared his own concerns with her and asked her to pray for him. To make things even better, Peter went to Teresa's spiritual directors and assured them of the validity of her experiences. After that, she said, they "stopped frightening me so much."[6]

Thus was Teresa empowered. In trusting her prayer to God alone and in finding a prayerful human friend who truly understood her, she indeed became a changed person. She was free. Now she scorned the devils she had once so feared. As she began the great works of the last twenty years of her life, she proclaimed:

*Not a fig do I care for all the devils in hell. It is they who
will fear me! "Oh, the devil! The devil!" we say, when
instead we could say, "God! God!" and make the devil
tremble. I am sure I fear those who are terrified of the devil
more than I fear the devil himself. For the devil cannot harm
me at all, but they, especially if they are confessors, can
upset people a great deal.*[7]

Teresa expressed her experience of empowerment
in many ways in her writings. I believe one of her
poems says it especially beautifully:

Nada te turbe;	Let nothing disturb you;
nada te espante;	Let nothing make you afraid;
todo se pasa;	All things pass;
Dios no se muda,	But God is unchanging,
la paciencia	Patience
todo lo alcanza.	is enough for everything.
Quien a Dios tiene,	You who have God
nada le falta.	lack nothing.
Solo Dios basta.	God alone is sufficient.[8]

In Teresa's experience thus far, we can see some of
the fundamental characteristics of the dark night of
the soul. I will explain these further as we proceed,

but here we can note that during many of her long struggles Teresa was confused about what was happening. She did not trust her inner sense of prayer, believing it could as well be coming from the devil as from God. To use another word, things were *obscure.* This is the root meaning of the Spanish word *oscura,* translated as "dark," as in *noche oscura,* "dark night." As in the dark of a real night, Teresa could not see clearly. At the same time, she was very attached to the opinions of others, her friends as well as her counselors. Not knowing whom to believe only compounded her confusion. Only when she was liberated from this attachment—through no achievement of her own—was she able to trust her own inner authenticity in prayer. Finally, she put her ultimate trust in God alone.

Such obscurity and attachment, followed by God-given clarity, liberation of love, and deepening of faith, are consistent hallmarks of the dark night of the soul.[9] Often, this liberation results in a remarkable release of creative activity in the world. This is especially obvious in Teresa's case. Once paralyzed by uncertainty and self-doubt, she went on to become the major reformer of the Carmelite order—truly a force to be reckoned with.

The Reform

Peter of Alcántara died only two years later, but not before he encouraged Teresa to begin the work that would occupy the rest of her life: the Carmelite reform. Years before, Peter had begun a reform of his own within the Franciscan order, advocating a return to a simpler and more austere lifestyle. Such reforms had been happening in a number of different religious orders in Europe. Like the others, the new Franciscan communities that followed Peter were called *discalced,* "without shoes," to reflect their calling to greater austerity.

Teresa herself had been thinking about what a discalced movement might bring to Carmelite life. The Order of Our Lady of Mount Carmel had begun late in the twelfth century in the Palestinian desert, with a small group of hermits living a life of simplicity and solitude in caves and huts on the slopes of Mount Carmel. By Teresa's time however, the Carmelite rule had changed. Although still austere by our modern standards, Carmelite rule placed little emphasis on solitude and interior prayer, and convents and monasteries often contained hundreds of people. Some two hundred lived in Teresa's own Convent of the Incarnation in Ávila; wealthier nuns occupied suites of rooms that also housed relatives and even servants. Although prayers went on continually, they were nearly always simply recited. There was little or no instruction in quiet prayer and very few opportunities for solitude.[10]

Reflecting on the simplicity of the old desert life, Teresa and a few of her friends began to wonder about forming a new convent that would contain only about a dozen nuns and be organized more along the lines of the original Carmelite rule. Then one day in prayer, Teresa heard God telling her to proceed. The tiny new house was to be named for St. Joseph, whose intercession Teresa was sure had cured her. She wrote Peter of Alcántara about the idea and subsequently met with him to discuss it. He consistently encouraged her and gave her much practical advice. But her ideas met with widespread opposition as soon as they became public. Teresa called it a "great persecution," consisting of "gossip, derision, and being called crazy."[11]

But Teresa's newfound self-confidence in God prevailed, and in 1562 she founded the first house of her reform, the Monastery of St. Joseph in Ávila. It was less than two months later that Peter died. Teresa said she thought God had kept him alive long enough to assist her with the foundation. Even after he died, she had several visions of him in which he continued to give her advice and encouragement.[12]

Teresa became prioress of the new little convent and lived there for five years, "the most restful years of my life." Having finished writing her *Life*, she wrote two more significant works during this time: *The Way of Perfection* and *Meditations on the Song of Songs*. In early 1567, the Carmelite prior general, Juan Rubeo, visited St. Joseph's and told Teresa of his desire for more such reformed religious houses, for men as well as women. He sent her to found a second house in Medina del Campo and, ultimately, fifteen more convents.[13]

Teresa knew at the outset that, if the houses for nuns were to succeed, monasteries for men must also be established. Rubeo gave her permission to found two houses for men, and Teresa began to pray fervently for "at least one friar" to help her with this work.[14]

Teresa and John Meet

Teresa's prayers were answered promptly. She discovered her first friar upon her arrival in Medina del Campo. The local prior, Fray Antonio, assured Teresa of his desire for a simpler life. To this end, he had been planning to join the very austere Carthusian order. Instead, he agreed to help Teresa in her reform. A few weeks later, Teresa met a second friar who also had been thinking of joining the Carthusians. This was John of the Cross.[15]

It was the fall of 1567. Teresa was fifty-two years old. John was twenty-five and newly ordained. For the previous three years he had been studying and teaching at the prestigious university in Salamanca. He had returned to Medina del Campo to say his first Mass when Teresa heard of him and arranged a meeting.

Several things about John immediately struck Teresa. One was his size—he was less than five feet tall. Teresa later made frequent lighthearted references to John's stature, referring to him as *"mi Senequita,"* "my little Seneca," or *"santico,"* the "little saint." After convincing him to join her reform work, she reportedly wrote to a friend that she now had "a friar and a half."[16] The brilliance of John's intellect and the sincerity of his prayer also impressed Teresa. She said of this first meeting, "I liked him very much. . . . Small in stature though he may be, I believe he is great in the sight of God."[17]

Teresa quickly convinced John that he did not have to leave the Carmelites to find a more contemplative life. Instead, he could work with Teresa and establish discalced houses for men. From what we know of Teresa at that time, it would have been very difficult to say no to her. But John was not at all reluctant. He returned to Salamanca just long enough to finish his studies and became Teresa's apprentice the following summer. Within a year, the first house of the reform for men came into being in Duruelo.

Working together, John and Teresa developed a rich complementarity. They each saw in the other something they felt was missing in themselves. Although well educated for a woman of her time, Teresa was painfully conscious of lacking the formal theological and intellectual training that was available only to men. She valued "men of learning" highly and was deeply impressed by John's brilliant intellect.

She saw in John's mind the capacity to explain many of the concepts she had so struggled and fumbled over in her own writing.

For his part, John had come to believe that the intellect was considerably overrated. In today's idiom, he had been there and done that. He was convinced that understanding and reason could do no more than point in the general direction of spiritual reality. It was direct spiritual experience that he valued most, and Teresa had a wealth of it. She immediately became his spiritual mother, nourishing him with her images and visions of the spiritual life. She was initially frustrated with John's devaluing of the intellect and kept encouraging him to use it. In turn, his interest in her experience must have been a source of reassurance to her.

The relationship between Teresa and John was mutually enriching, but they remained who they were. John could not help being a serious intellectual ascetic, and no amount of conceptual stimulation could change Teresa's irrepressible earthiness, practicality, and humor. In a playful response to a treatise John wrote in late 1576 Teresa said, "God deliver me from people so spiritual that they want to turn everything into perfect contemplation, no matter what!"[18]

Above all, Teresa and John shared a relentless, burning passion for God, a wellspring of spiritual desire that never ran dry. Within ten years, John would find this passion leading him into another, deeper meaning of the word "passion": suffering.

A Dark Night for John

I n sixteenth-century Spain there was little separation of church and state as we understand it today. Jurisdictions of political and religious authority were mixed, confused, and frequently determined by violence. In this atmosphere, religious orders handled most of their own judicial matters. They had their own legal and penal systems, and it was not uncommon for monasteries to maintain men-at-arms and prisons. This was nothing new for John, but he never expected that he himself would become an outlaw.

In 1572 John had gone to Teresa's original Convent of the Incarnation in Ávila as a confessor to the nuns. He gained much experience in spiritual direction there and produced a few writings, which, sadly, have been lost. Three years later, an Italian Carmelite edict

drafted to oppose the reform made it unlawful for
him to remain there. However, the papal nuncio (the
pope's official representative to the court of King
Philip II) ordered John to stay on at the Incarnation.
John obeyed what he felt was the proper authority
and in so doing became a Carmelite criminal.

The "Friars of the Observance" (the unreformed,
or "calced," friars) were now mobilizing strongly
against the reform. They briefly apprehended John in
early 1576, but released him when the nuncio inter-
vened. In the summer of 1577, however, the nuncio
died and the attacks on the reform intensified.
Jerónimo Gracián, Teresa's dearest male friend,
came under such vilification that Teresa wrote to
King Philip on his behalf. Fifty-five nuns were excom-
municated because they had voted for Teresa to be
their prioress at the Convent of the Incarnation.
Then, during the night of December 2, 1577, men
broke into John's residence at the Incarnation,
abducted him and another friar, and took them
bound and blindfolded to the monastery in Toledo.[19]

There, after multiple beatings, during which he
consistently refused to disavow his work with Teresa's
reform, John was confined in the monastery prison.
Hearing of his plight, Teresa immediately sent

another letter to King Philip, begging him to intervene and expressing great fear for John's life.[20]

The friars in Toledo subjected John to extreme abuse and deprivation, feeding him only bread, water, and an occasional sardine. He was not allowed to bathe or change clothes. He regularly underwent the "circular discipline," during which the monks took turns flogging him. After two months, they put him in solitary confinement in a tiny cell with only a slit in the wall for light and air.

There, in the dark of the prison, John began to compose his great poetic works. At first he created them mentally and memorized them. Later, a new and more compassionate jailer allowed him writing materials and even let him out to stretch and see the sun for brief periods. Thus he was able to write down, among some other verses, the majority of his first great poem, *The Spiritual Canticle*.

Then on one very real dark night, after nine months of imprisonment, John escaped. There are varying stories of how he accomplished it. Some say it was a miracle. Others say friends helped him. The most reliable account is that he managed his own escape, laboriously loosening the screws on his cell door and making a rope out of bedding.[21]

He staggered to a nearby discalced convent. The nuns there secretly took him to a hospital, where he received treatment for extreme malnutrition. Upon recovery, he made his way south, where the discalced Carmelites were more independent. There he continued his work with the reform, founding more houses and a college. He continued giving spiritual direction. And he continued writing.

The Writings of Teresa and John

Teresa and John are well known in the Western world as great mystical authors. Both have been named Doctors of the Church because of their exemplary contributions to religious understanding. What is less known is that both were accomplished poets, and that John is the patron saint of Spanish poetry. Some call him Spain's greatest poet.

Like the biblical Song of Songs, which so inspired both Teresa and John, John's poetry is romantic, erotic, and full of sensual imagery. His three great poems—*The Spiritual Canticle, The Dark Night,* and *The Living Flame of Love*—are devoid of explicit religious language. Copies of the poems were circulated widely among the discalced Carmelites, and it is not surprising that he was asked to explain the meaning of the verses. In response to such requests, John composed the commentaries that comprise the great bulk of his extant writing.

For many generations, people were exposed to these commentaries, often unfortunately to the exclusion of the poetry itself. As a result, John has often been seen as intellectually abstract, austere, and overly ascetic. Taken out of context, a small portion of his work does sound that way. But his poetry attests that nothing could be further from the truth. The poems are hymns of the grandeur of human existence, full of passion, rich in yearning and joy, vibrant with the beauty of creation. John himself says repeatedly that his poetry is the most direct possible expression of his experience, and his commentaries at best can only shed "vague light" on the poems—much less on the actual experiences that inspired them.[22]

It is impossible for anyone to adequately express the deep movements of love within the spiritual life. It cannot be done by words, by art, or by any way other than the love with which one lives one's life. At the same time, though, I must say that I have never seen such magnificent attempts as those of Teresa and John. Today, as I read their words from more than four centuries ago, I often feel as though they are not only saying what I am feeling, but also *explaining* it, setting it in context and giving it a meaning that is consistently reassuring and encouraging. Obviously and rightly, not everyone feels this way. As different as their personalities were, Teresa and John shared a spiritual style that not everyone is drawn to. Both were quick to affirm that other people may well be called to other ways. "God," Teresa says, "does not lead everyone along the same path."[23]

Nevertheless, there is wisdom in Teresa and John's legacy that bridges spiritual orientations as well as spans cultures and centuries. Teresa's psychological insights compare favorably with those of Freud and his twentieth-century followers. John's descriptions of attachment brilliantly enhance modern addiction theory. Their imagery has a universal quality that speaks to the hearts of today's spiritual seekers. From a contemporary perspective, we can easily see Teresa's growth as a woman in the progression of her writings, from the lowliness with which she described herself in early works to the inner beauty she depicted in *The Interior Castle*. And although the

Scholastic theology that prevailed in their time might now seem dated, there is also much that can strike modern readers as refreshing. In some ways, Teresa and John might even be accused of "New Age" tendencies. Teresa, for example, speaks readily of hell and the devils, but her concern is more for a hell created on earth than the eternal damnation so feared in her time. And although John can sound dualistic in using such classical terms as "natural" and "supernatural," he can also make a statement so holistic that it is radical even by today's standards: *"El centro del alma es Dios,"* "The center of the soul *is* God."[24]

It is to this place, this holy center of each human soul, that we now turn our attention as we begin to explore the profound spiritual wisdom that Teresa and John have given us.

CHAPTER TWO

WE ARE LOVE

The Theology of Teresa and John

Here's the thing, say Shug. The thing I believe. God is inside you and inside everybody else. You come into the world with God. But only them that search for it inside find it. And sometimes it just manifest itself even if you not looking, or don't know what you're looking for. Trouble do it for most folks, I think. Sorrow, lord.

—*Alice Walker*[1]

John and Teresa shared powerful convictions about human nature in relationship to God. These convictions colored all their images and writings, so it is important to understand them. Because John was so intellectually precise, I will rely extensively on his writings in this chapter. By and large, though, this theology belongs to both John and Teresa. Most of John's images, symbols, and wisdom can be found first in Teresa's work. In many cases, it seems as though John has taken what Teresa has taught him and put it into sophisticated theological language.

Person, Soul, and God

When Teresa and John speak of the soul, they are not talking about something a person *has*, but who a person most deeply *is:* the essential spiritual nature of a human being. They use "person" when speaking casually, but whenever they are dealing with spiritual matters, they nearly always use "soul" instead. For them, the soul is not a separate part or aspect of a person, but rather what you see when you look at a person with spiritual eyes.[2]

Similarly, Teresa and John speak expediently of finding God and growing toward union with God. They do not believe this is something that can really be achieved, however, for the simple reason that union with God already exists. Everyone always has been and always will be in union with God. This union is so deep and complete that seeking God must include self-knowledge, and self-knowledge must include the search for God. Teresa heard God's voice in prayer saying, "Seek yourself in Me, and in yourself seek Me."[3]

As did St. Augustine twelve centuries earlier, Teresa and John maintain that God is closer to us than we are to our very selves. We are born in union with God and we "live and move and have our being" in God throughout our lives (Acts 17:28). In keeping with the root meaning of "nature" (*natura*, "birth"), this union with the Divine *is* our human nature. It is so essential to our being that John says we could not exist without it.[4]

Moreover, this essential unity applies not just to saints or the pure of heart, not only to Christians, and not even only to human beings. To quote John directly, "To understand this union of which we speak, know that God is present in substance in each soul, even that of the greatest sinner in the world. And this kind of union with God always exists, in all creatures."[5]

A Journey of Consciousness

The problem for most of us is that we don't *realize* how united we are with God. Except in rare moments of mystical experience, most of us don't generally feel such intimacy with the Divine. Even if we believe devoutly that God is present with us, our usual experience is that we are "here" and God is "there," loving and gracious perhaps, but irrevocably separate. "We just don't understand ourselves," says Teresa, "or know who we are."[6]

At worst, we give lip service to God's presence, but then feel and act as if we were completely on our own. I think of church committee meetings, pastoral counseling sessions, or even spiritual direction meetings I have attended. They often begin with a sincere prayer, "God, be with us *(as if God might be in attendance at another meeting)* and guide our decisions and our actions." Then at the end comes, "Amen," and the door crashes shut on God-attentiveness. Now we have said our prayers and it is time to get down to business. The modern educator Parker Palmer calls this "functional atheism . . . the belief that ultimate responsibility for everything rests with me."[7]

There are many reasons why we fail to recognize our deep and irrevocable communion with the Divine. Some are simply defensive. A direct experience of union or deep intimacy may be beautiful beyond words, but it also requires a certain sacrifice of our self-image as separate and distinct. We become vulnerable, less in control. We can no longer maintain the illusion that we are the master of our destiny. Other reasons are inherent in our dualistic way of thinking. As soon as we use the label "God" or "divine presence," we make an object of it, separate from ourselves. Taken together, these reasons encourage us to dwell in the more comfortable, controllable world of "God and me," rather than the vague, vulnerable realm of "God in me and I in God." Clinging to the "God and me" mentality, we actually come to believe such bogus sayings as "God helps those who help themselves" or "Pray as if everything depended on God, but work as if everything depended on yourself."[8]

At the same time, there is a certain authenticity in viewing God as distinct from oneself. Such a perspective not only acknowledges the irrevocable beyondness and incomprehensibility of the Divine, but it also permits us to have a sense of *relationship* with God. It allows for what Teresa and John saw as the dynamic love affair between lover and Beloved, the soul and God.

Teresa and John maintain that the human mind can never grasp the real truth of God; it is always beyond us. Any conclusion or image we come to about God, no matter how wise, will always remain incomplete. Thus there can be no clear right and wrong about how one views one's relationship with the Divine. "God and me" has its truth, as does "God in me" and even "God *as* me." Any of these taken by itself, however, leads to distortion. And even taken all together, they still are incomplete.

Thus when Teresa and John use phrases like "seeking God" or "finding union with God," they are speaking to the "God and me" mentality. On the surface, such phrases seem to indicate an actual lessening of distance between a person and God. But since we cannot really grow any closer to God than we already are, the words actually refer to a deepening *realization* of the intimacy and union that already exists.

The spiritual life for Teresa and John has nothing to do with actually getting closer to God. It is instead

a journey of *consciousness*. Union with God is neither
acquired nor received; it is *realized,* and in that sense
it is something that can be yearned for, sought after,
and—with God's grace—found.

According to John, it takes love to realize this
union; it happens *in* love, and however deep the realization is, it results in more love. In this manner, John
says the soul "*arrives* at perfect union with God
through love."[9] This deepening of love is the real
purpose of the dark night of the soul. The dark night
helps us become who we are created to be: lovers of
God and one another.

John says the soul is in God like a stone buried
in the earth. In a way, the stone and the earth are
already at one and, in a manner of speaking, the
stone is already in the earth's center. Yet there are
many "centers" in the earth, and the stone can
always sink more deeply, closer to the earth's "deepest
center." Thus the relationship between God and
person is dynamic, always capable of greater deepening. More than a century before Isaac Newton
explained gravity, John said that the soul is attracted
to the deepest center of God like the stone is attracted
to the deepest center of the earth—and that this
attraction is mutual. The force of attraction between

the soul and the center of God, however, is not gravity. It is love.[10]

Love at the Core

As far as I know, only one place in the Bible explains why God created human beings. The apostle Paul, preaching to the Greeks in Athens, says that God created us "so that we might seek God . . . and find God" (Acts 17:27). To my knowledge, neither Teresa nor John specifically cites this reference, but their theology is in deep harmony with it. Clearly, it exemplifies their understanding of human nature. If the purpose of our existence is to seek and find God, then there is a seed of desire in each of us, a fundamental motivation, a basic longing for the fulfillment of that purpose. Again with St. Augustine, John and Teresa would both affirm that "Thou hast made us for Thyself, and our hearts are restless until they rest in Thee."[11]

According to this theology, we are not only born with God at our center, but we are also born with a heart full of desire for God. This yearning is our fundamental motive force; it *is* the human spirit. It is the energy behind everything we seek and aspire to. And if indeed we are in intimate union with God in the center, then the soul's desire is God's desire. The soul's love for God is God's love for the soul.

This love and desire represent something far deeper than simple emotions. They reflect humanity's most profound *motivation*. Socrates and Plato might have called it *eros*, the fundamental motivation toward ultimate truth and beauty. Some theologians see it as the essence of the human spirit: the "radical incompleteness" that determines the basic direction in which our life energy moves.

People express and experience this foundational love force in unique combinations of ways. Many actually have a strong emotional sense of it, as John and Teresa express in their "bridal mysticism" that speaks so much of lover and Beloved. Others might experience it less as feeling and more as commitment to goodness, seeking truth, or appreciating beauty. Still others have no conscious sense of it at all. In moments of quiet reflection, they may know that something is propelling them toward fulfillment, but they would be at a loss to explain it further.

Regardless of how or whether we experience our fundamental motivations, Teresa and John's theology maintains that all of us are both living physical expressions *of* God's love and deep capacities *for* God's love. Human beings are, in a way, embodiments of the scriptural affirmation that we love because God first loved us (1 John 4:19). At the same time, in the divine reality that unites us all, we are living potential fulfillments of the two great commandments: to love God with our whole being, and our neighbors as ourselves. "Those who do not love their neighbors," Teresa prays, "do not love You, my Lord."[12]

Very simply, love is the core of everything in the theology of Teresa and John. It is the sole purpose of all creation and of us as human beings. And it is, finally, impossible to distinguish precisely whether this love at our center is our love of God, or God's love of us, or our love of ourselves and one another, or God's love of God. In the final stanza of John's last great poem, the lover speaks to the Beloved: "How tenderly and gently you awaken within my heart." In the commentary, he tries to delineate exactly who it is that is awakening, but the essential unity prevents him. Indeed, our souls are asleep to the truth until God's love awakens them, he says, but since all things arise from God, "our awakening is God's awakening."[13]

In summary, all human beings are created in and from the love of God, with an inborn love for God that continually arises from God and constantly seeks God. This love is meant to flow for all people and all creation. This is our true human nature. It is who we are.

At this point, one might reasonably ask, if we're made of love, filled with love, and meant for love, why do we feel so separate and behave so destructively? According to John and Teresa, there are two fundamental reasons. The first we have already mentioned: we are asleep to the truth; we do not realize who we are and what we are for. The second reason is that we misplace our love; we become attached to things other than God. To understand how this happens, we need to look in greater depth at the way Teresa and John envision the human soul.

Soul Circles

Although not drawn as such, Teresa's and John's images of the soul take the shape of circles. Late in her life, Teresa described the soul as a beautiful interior castle with seven inner mansions, or dwelling places, each of which contains many rooms.

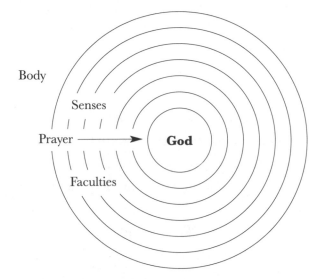

We might visualize this soul castle as seven concentric circles. God, of course, dwells in the center. Although I cannot draw it on paper, God also surrounds and permeates the castle. In Teresa's imagery, the castle's outer wall is the body. The physical senses (sight, hearing, touch, etc.) are the people who live in the castle. The guards and caretakers of the castle are the person's faculties: intellect, memory, will, and imagination. (Teresa says they don't do a very good job.)[14]

As Teresa describes it, the process of the spiritual life consists of an inward journey in which a person's consciousness moves from the outer, sensory realm toward God at the inmost center. Prayer is the doorway through which one's consciousness enters the castle, and the path along which it proceeds to the center.

John's portrayal reflects the Scholastic theology in which he was trained. Again, God is at the center, as well as surrounding and permeating the soul. John differentiates between an outer, "sensory" aspect of the soul and an inner, "spiritual" one. As we shall see, he divides the dark night of the soul into two corresponding phases: the dark night of the senses and the dark night of the spirit.[15]

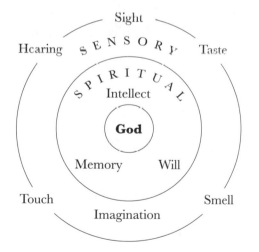

The outer, sensory dimension of the soul includes the five physical senses, which John sees as the soul's windows to the physical world. The imagination, although a deeper function, includes many physical qualities and can be visualized as a borderland between the spiritual and sensory aspects.

The inner, spiritual aspect of the soul contains the three spiritual faculties of the human being: intellect, memory, and will. The intellect meant much the same to John as it does to us today: the capacity to think rationally, to understand and comprehend. The will also has a familiar meaning: the capacity to make choices, form intentions, and direct actions. The memory, however, meant something richer for John than for most of us today. In John's thinking, memory is not just a storehouse for past experience; based on the past, it also fuels the imagination in looking to the future. Memory is the ground of dreaming.

Nada

It is important here to reiterate that Teresa and John see each soul as a living desire for God. God is love, and God creates every person out of love and because of love, for the purpose of love. We may be unaware of it, but we are all born with a natural and lifelong yearning for the fulfillment of love. "At the end of the day," John says, "you will be examined in love."[16] Inasmuch as the whole person is an embodiment of love's desire for fulfillment, each aspect of the person, each sense and faculty, is also filled with that desire. To use John's language, each sense and faculty of the soul is an "appetite" for God.[17]

Thus every part of us is, at its core, a desire for love's fulfillment. Though we seldom recognize it, our senses seek the beauty, the sweetness, the good feelings of God. Our mind seeks the truth and wisdom of God. Our will seeks to live out the goodness, the righteousness of God. Our memory and imagination seek the justice and peace of God. In other words, we yearn for the attributes of God with every part of ourselves. Human beings are two-legged, walking, talking desires for God.

Ultimately, it is only God's very self that can truly satisfy our deepest desires and liberate our love for all of life. The frustration arises because our senses and other capacities are limited in what they can apprehend, and God's true nature is always beyond them.

The best they can do is reflect some image or concept of God, some brief glimpse seen "through a glass darkly" (1 Cor. 13:12). God is at once too immanently at one with us and too transcendently beyond us to be fully felt or appreciated in any normal way. John goes on to say that God's true attributes are too perfect, too pure, and too delicate for any of our faculties to grasp.[18]

To put it another way, all our capacities are geared toward appreciating *objects of attention:* sense perceptions, images, ideas, memories, emotions, fantasies, and so on. We always expect to be aware of some *thing.* But God is too intimate to be an object, too ultimate to be a thing. Our faculties can only comprehend the *things of* God, like the beauty of creation, the goodness of the attraction we feel for others, or the glimpses of truth we experience in religious images and concepts. All these things may reflect or represent God to us, but they miss the essence of God. To our normal human capacities God is *nada,* "no-thing."[19]

Somewhere around 1579, shortly after his escape, John drew a sketch of paths up a mountain to portray the spiritual life. Along these paths, the soul seeks God in all kinds of good things, but finds repeatedly that God is "not this, not that." Even at the top of the mountain, God is no-thing, *nada*.[20]

No matter how hard we try, our senses cannot savor God's ultimate sweetness directly. We cannot see God with our eyes, face-to-face. Our minds cannot comprehend God's wisdom. We cannot will ourselves into God's perfect goodness. Even our most inventive imagination can come up with only symbols and representations that stand for the Reality we desire.

It might seem cruel for God to create us to love God and then to seem so elusive. At the beginning of John's *Spiritual Canticle,* the bride (soul) cries out to her lover (God), "You fled like a deer after wounding me, and I went out, calling for you, and you were gone." Teresa and John refer to this tantalizing frustration in many ways. John calls it God's games; Teresa calls it war. For both, it is the "wound of love." Both also affirm, however, that the entire enterprise and experience of human life is neither cruel nor antagonistic; it is nothing other than love doing what love does: yearning, seeking, creating, liberating, and always coming alive.[21]

Most of us, most of the time, don't feel this degree of existential frustration. We are blessed by ignorance. We don't have a clue about what is really going on.

Attachment and Idolatry

Although we are all born with a fundamental desire for God and the fullness of love, most of us don't know it. The true nature of the desire remains unconscious, often for a very long time. As Teresa says, we simply don't know who we are. It's different for each person of course, but most of us begin with what seem like the very simple desires to experience pleasure and avoid pain. This alone can provide plenty of motivation for a rich experience of life, and we generally remain occupied with seeking happiness, gratification, and success, completely unaware of our deeper, divine motivations.

To complicate matters, Western culture teaches us that we should be able to achieve perfect satisfaction in life through our own capacities and efforts. Indeed, for many years we can feel very fulfilled in our search for enjoyable experiences, loving relationships, and rewarding work. Even if we are not completely satisfied, we can at least be preoccupied with our efforts. We grasp and embrace what we can. We achieve what is possible. In the process we taste of beauty, truth, goodness, and meaning, and the tastes keep us going.

Because we can't encounter God directly through our senses and concepts, we are naturally drawn to the things we *can* feel and see and grasp. We gravitate to the things *of* God, to things that we sense as good, true, beautiful, and loving. We expect these good things to satisfy us. We do not realize that we love them not for themselves, but because they whisper to us of their Creator, the One we really long for. We do not yet know what Teresa and John discovered, that such things are only "messengers," and that our love, even for them, cannot be free without the grace of their Creator.[22]

Usually we do not have a clue that we are drawn to such things because something deep in us senses the God-ness in them. All we know is that we desire good feelings and want to avoid unpleasantness. The more goodness we experience, the more we want. Thus we become conditioned. We live, in large part, on the basis of habit. To a certain extent, habits are healthy and natural processes. Habits generally lead us to take care of ourselves and our loved ones, to learn and to be creative, and to accomplish good things. But there are also some drawbacks.

First, some of our habits inevitably become choiceless. They turn into compulsions. Compulsions are

not good for the soul. Some, like racism or vengefulness, are clearly destructive. Others, like overwork or
zealous self-sacrifice, may appear admirable on the
surface, but devour us interiorly. Regardless of how a
compulsion appears externally, underneath it is always
robbing us of our freedom. We act not because we
have chosen to, but because we have to. We cling to
things, people, beliefs, and behaviors not because we
love them, but because we are terrified of losing
them.

The classical spiritual term for this compulsive
condition is *attachment*. The word comes from old
European roots meaning "staked" or "nailed to." All
major spiritual traditions have long understood that
attachment binds the energy of the human spirit
to something other than love. Each of us has countless attachments. We are attached to our daily rou-
tines, our environments, our relationships, and of
course our possessions. We are also attached to
our religious beliefs and to our images of ourselves,
others, and God.

Attachments are inevitable. Our brains learn by
developing habits, many of which become choiceless
attachments. We depend upon attachments to pre-
determine behavior so we don't have to think through

each situation afresh. Without these unchosen habits, we would be paralyzed. In this way, most of our attachments work well for us, and we are generally unaware of how they compromise our freedom.

Sooner or later, however, we are bound to discover that some of our attachments are not so efficient. They get in our way. Like the apostle Paul, we find ourselves doing what we don't want to do and not doing what we most desire (Rom. 7:15). We call these unpleasant attachments "bad habits." When we consider them very bad, when we see how they hinder our love, we call them *addictions*. Just as we all have attachments, we all have addictions. In many cases, it is addiction of one form or another that finally brings us to realize how far we have strayed from our true desire. In so doing, it brings us to our knees.[23]

In a spiritual sense, the objects of our attachments and addictions become *idols*. We give them our time, energy, and attention whether we want to or not, even—and often especially—when we are struggling to rid ourselves of them. We want to be free, compassionate, and happy, but in the face of our attachments we are clinging, grasping, and fearfully self-absorbed.

This is the root of our trouble. Our birth legacy, our human nature, is the fulfillment of the promise of the two great commandments: we *will* love God with all our heart and soul and mind, and we *will* love one another as ourselves (Matt. 22:37–39). Yet we find our hearts are given elsewhere, our souls compelled by something else, our minds kidnapped by other things. Whether we admit or deny it, we are worshiping false gods. Most of the time, we try to deny it.

CHAPTER THREE

A DEEPER LONGING

The Liberation of Desire

Heaven is to be
in God at last made free.

—*Evelyn Underhill*[1]

Denial, as some recovering alcoholics say, is more than just a river in Egypt. Psychoanalysts categorize denial as one of the most primitive ways we have of defending against stress. If something is too painful or embarrassing, our minds simply refuse to accept it. Such is often the case with attachment. Attachment thrives on denial. Spiritually, denial is a two-headed demon. It keeps our idolatry out of our awareness, allowing us to believe that our capacity for love is full and free. Simultaneously, it buries our true desire for love, convincing us that life consists of willful dedication to achieving our own satisfaction. We all engage in denial of some sort. We do it because it works, and sometimes it works for a very long time.

For all of us, however, there are moments of dawning awareness, little cracks in our armor that reveal glimpses of our deeper longing and our true nature. We generally don't like what we see there, because it forces us to admit we are fundamentally dissatisfied. We begin to see that the results of our efforts are not quite as perfect as we had hoped for. Perhaps the career we worked so hard to achieve is not as rewarding as we'd expected. Maybe the love relationship we thought would make us complete has become timeworn and frayed. Things that gave us pleasure in the past may now seem empty. Such glimpses occur in unique ways for each person, but they always happen. They happen repeatedly. Each time, they represent a twilight of the dark night of the soul.

Early in life it is often possible to shut out these momentary dissatisfactions as soon as they appear. We can blame them on a bad mood, tough circumstances, or a lousy day. We can assume things will be better tomorrow. With more maturity, however, we may begin to admit that we've been off target in our strivings and have missed the satisfaction we'd expected. Even then, we often think we can adjust our course, renew our efforts, and eventually win out. In the middle of life, we begin to sense our time is limited; changes need to be more radical if we're going to find what we want before we're too old to enjoy it. Still later in life we may finally be more open to acceptance. Perhaps what we've been after all along have been only appetizers, "messengers." Maybe we've been grasping for good things when what we've really desired is the Creator of all good things.

Not uncommonly this dawning awareness happens intermittently over the course of a lifetime, as I have described it. But it can happen at any time. Some people even seem to have been born with it. They grow up trying to adjust themselves to the values and strivings that surround them, but somehow their hearts are never in it. They have a deep awareness that fulfillment cannot be found through acquisition and achievement. They often feel like misfits because of the different, deeper, ungraspable love they feel inside them. For them, the journey is not so much toward realization of their desire as toward being able to claim the desire they already have in a culture that neither understands nor supports it.

The awareness can happen in infancy, old age, or anytime in between. And it can happen anywhere along the spectrum of pain and pleasure. It can be very pleasant, as in the simple grace of realizing what it is that one really desires. Or it can be exquisitely painful, as in the sudden loss of what one loves or the despairing realization that what one has given oneself to is fundamentally empty and meaningless. And almost always, such realizations are surrounded by confusion.

The Darkness

B rother Lawrence of the Resurrection, another Carmelite mystic, lived in seventeenth-century France. At one point in his famous treatise, *The Practice of the Presence of God*, he says, "People would be surprised if they knew what their souls said to God sometimes."[2] Centuries before Freud "discovered" the unconscious, contemplatives such as Brother Lawrence, Teresa, and John had a profound appreciation that there is an active life of the soul that goes on beneath our awareness. It is to this unconscious dimension of the spiritual life that Teresa and John refer when they use the term "dark."

When we speak of darkness today, we are often referring to something sinister, as in "powers of darkness" or the "dark side." As I've said before, this is not what Teresa and John mean when they used the Spanish word for dark, *oscura*. For them, it simply means "obscure." In the same way that things are difficult to see at night, the deepest relationship between God and person is hidden from our conscious awareness.

In speaking of *la noche oscura,* the dark night of the soul, John is addressing something mysterious and unknown, but by no means sinister or evil. It is instead profoundly sacred and precious beyond all imagining. John says the dark night of the soul is "happy," "glad," "guiding," and full of "absolute grace." It is the secret way in which God not only liberates us from our attachments and idolatries, but also brings us to the realization of our true nature. The night is the means by which we find our heart's desire, our freedom for love.

This is not to say that all darkness is good. Teresa and John use another word, *tinieblas,* to describe the more sinister kind of darkness. There is no doubt about the difference. Teresa uses *oscura* in saying that the spiritual life is so dark she needs much patience "in order to write about what I don't know." But she uses *tinieblas* when she says, "The devil is darkness itself."[3] Similarly, John says it is one thing to be in *oscuras* and quite another to be in *tinieblas*. In *oscuras* things are hidden; in *tinieblas* one is blind. In fact, it is the very blindness of *tinieblas*, our slavery to attachment and delusion, that the dark night of the soul is working to heal.[4]

Suffering and Joy

For Teresa and John, the dark night of the soul is a totally loving, healing, and liberating process. Whether it *feels* that way is another question entirely. Nowadays most people think of the dark night of the soul as a time of suffering and tribulation—redemptive perhaps, but entirely unpleasant. This is not always the case.

The only characteristic of the experience of the dark night that is certain is its obscurity. One simply does not comprehend clearly what is happening.

Some dark-night experiences, as I have indicated, may be quite pleasant. One friend of mine, driven by unrelenting perfectionism, had dedicated his adult life to doing everything right. He had a sense of humor, and we had good times together, but it hurt to see the pain his self-judgment was causing him. Then, gradually and inexplicably, he felt himself relaxing. He was delightfully liberated from his burdensome sense of responsibility; he was "free just to be," as he put it. Although he wasn't sure what was going on and at times wondered if he might just be getting lazy, his overall experience of the change was joyful.

For another person in another situation, the same kind of liberation might be very painful. When I was practicing psychiatry, a woman came to see me for depression. She had spent her life taking care of her family, frequently neglecting her own interests in the process. She felt guilty about anything she did for herself. She struggled with a sense of emptiness after her children had grown up and was later devastated to discover that her husband was having an affair. The experience was beginning to ease her care-taking compulsion, but it certainly did not feel like liberation. All she felt was pain, loss, and abandonment. Glimpses of her growing freedom made her even more depressed at first, because in relinquishing her total dedication to her marriage and family, she felt she was losing her only source of worth. Gradually, however, she began to enjoy time for herself. And in ways so subtle as to be almost unnoticeable amidst her pain, she began to feel a sense of meaning and value not for things she did, but just for who she was.

Liberation, whether experienced pleasurably or painfully, always involves relinquishment, some kind of *loss*. It may be a loss of something we're glad to be rid of, like a bad habit, or something we cling to for dear life, like a love relationship. Either way it's still a loss. Thus even when a dark-night experience is pleasant, there is still likely to be an accompanying sense of emptiness and perhaps even grief. Conversely, when a dark-night experience leaves us feeling tragically bereft, there still may be a sense of openness and fresh possibility. The point is, no matter how hard we try, we cannot see the process clearly. We only know what we're feeling at a given time, and that determines whether our experience is pleasurable or painful. As one of my friends often says, "God only knows what's really going on—literally!"

The Hidden Transformation

The obscurity of the dark night is so constant that I sometimes say, "If you're certain you're going through a dark night of the soul, you probably aren't!" The statement is flippant, but in my experience people having an experience of the dark night almost always think it is something else. If it's a pleasant experience, they may call it a mysterious breakthrough, a moment of unexplainable grace. If it is unpleasant, they tend to see it as a failure on their part: laziness, lassitude, resistance, or some other inadequacy.

If, as John maintains, the night is such a gift, why must the process remain so obscure? Since the night involves relinquishing attachments, it takes us beneath our denial into territory we are in the habit of avoiding. We might feel willing to relinquish compulsions we acknowledge as destructive, but anyone who has made a New Year's resolution knows how self-defeating such attempts can be. And what about the attachments we love, the ones we honor and value? Would we willingly cooperate in being freed from drivenness to do good works or to care for our family, even though we know it comes from compulsion rather than love? Would we willingly join God's grace in relinquishing attachments to the beliefs and images of God that give us comfort, security, and meaning, even if we recognize how they restrict and restrain us?

If we are honest, I think we have to admit that we will likely try to sabotage any movement toward true freedom. If we really knew what we were called to relinquish on this journey, our defenses would never allow us to take the first step. Sometimes the only way we can enter the deeper dimensions of the journey is by being unable to see where we're going.

John's explanation of the obscurity goes further. He says that in worldly matters it is good to have light so we know where to go without stumbling. But in spiritual matters it is precisely when we *do* think we know where to go that we are most likely to stumble. Thus, John says, God darkens our awareness *in order to keep us safe.* When we cannot chart our own course, we become vulnerable to God's protection, and the darkness becomes a "guiding night," a "night more kindly than the dawn."[5]

Let me say it again: whether we experience it as painful or pleasurable, *the night is dark for our protection.* We cannot liberate ourselves; our defenses and resis-

tances will not permit it, and we can hurt ourselves in
the attempt. To guide us toward the love that we most
desire, we must be *taken* where we could not and
would not go on our own. And lest we sabotage the
journey, we must not know where we are going. Deep
in the darkness, way beneath our senses, God is instilling "another, better love" and "deeper, more urgent
longings" that empower our willingness for all the
necessary relinquishments along the way.[6]

This transformative process—the freeing of love
from attachment—is akin to the ancient biblical concept of salvation. Hebrew words connoting salvation
often contain a root made of the letters *y* and *s*, *yodh*
and *shin*. One example is the Hebrew name of Jesus,
Yeshua, "God saves." This *y-s* root implies being set
free from bondage or confinement, enabled to move
freely, empowered to be and do according to one's
true nature. In contrast to life-denying asceticism
that advocates freedom *from* desire, Teresa and John
see authentic transformation as leading to freedom
for desire. For them, the essence of all human desire
is love.

In their understanding, the blindness of *tinieblas* is
enslavement to attachment and sin, an impoverishment
of love. Being "saved from sin," then, is synonymous

with being freed for the fullness of love. John, in the theology of his time, saw the transformative process of the dark night as identical to what supposedly occurred in purgatory—only it was happening now, during this life.

The goal of the transformation, the dawn after the night, consists of three precious gifts for the human soul. First, the soul's deepest desire is satisfied. Freed from the idolatries of their attachments, individuals are able to be completely in love with God and to love their neighbors as themselves. This love involves one's whole self: actions as well as feelings. Second, the delusion of separation from God and creation is dispelled; slowly one consciously realizes and enjoys the essential union that has always been present. Third, the freedom of love and realization of union leads to active participation *in* God. Here one not only recognizes one's own beauty and precious nature, but also shares God's love and compassion for others in real, practical service in the world.

When we begin to grasp the breadth and depth of this vision, it becomes obvious that we could never achieve it on our own. It seems a miracle that it could happen at all.

God and Person Together in the Night

We cannot achieve our own liberation or fulfillment; we would not even know where to begin. But neither does God reach down from the sky and manipulate us like puppets. Teresa and John maintain that God loves us far too much for that and will not invade where our hearts have closed the door. God, John says, is ultimately respectful of each soul, approaching it with deep regard according to its own unique needs and capacities. Teresa's way of putting it is that Christ "surrenders himself to us."[7]

So the process of the dark night is neither accomplished on our own nor worked within us by God alone. For Teresa and John, it is a mystical co-participation between God and person. With God as the center of the human soul it can be no other way.

Like so many things about the spiritual life, this co-participation is difficult to describe. Teresa and John frequently speak of *active* and *passive* dimensions of the spiritual life. They say, for example, that meditation is active while contemplation is passive.[8]

"Active" and "passive" were common theological terms of the time and a handy shorthand for John and Teresa, but they are easily misunderstood. It is especially important not to succumb to the simplistic interpretation that "active" is what we do and "passive" is what God does. Such misunderstandings have led to great confusion about the conduct of the spiritual life. For example, the arbitrary dualistic interpretation that human beings *do* meditation while God *gives* contemplation forced some desperate souls to come up with a special, lesser category of "acquired contemplation" that could be achieved through human effort alone. This idea was promulgated for at least two centuries and is still encountered in some circles today. A milder, more modern form of the same distortion is the assumption that active meditation practice somehow predisposes or opens an individual to be better ready to receive the gift of contemplation when God gives it. In my opinion, all such misunderstandings arise from slipping into the easy "God and me" mentality and failing to remember the unfathomable, mysteriously intimate co-participation of "God in me, I in God, God as me."[9]

Anyone who tries to describe the spiritual life in words is bound to overemphasize the "God and me" dimension. Given the inherent dualism of language, it becomes overwhelmingly complicated to always include the other, more mysterious dimensions of God-and-person. Besides, as we have discussed, most people do generally experience God as "other." Teresa and John, then, used active and passive as expedient descriptions of human experience. In this light, the active dimension of the spiritual life consists of what *feels* like one's own initiative, choice, or effort. The passive dimension *seems* to be more initiated and carried out by God.

Still, it is always important to remember that what is really happening is not so arbitrary. Often the perspective changes over time. Many mystics give accounts of having worked and struggled toward some spiritual goal, only to realize that when the goal is reached, it has come not as an achievement, but as a sheer gift. Even in theologies that assume an absolute separation between God and person, many would say that what seem to be our own best efforts and intentions exist only because they are first inspired by God. Regardless, our willingness for God's activity, our yes

to God, is always necessary, even though it may defy
description. It is in the soul's free and true yes to God,
John says, that God freely and truly gives the yes of
divine grace.[10]

John gives some powerful examples of how one's
own initiative and chosen willingness are critical even
in "passive" contemplation. An often quoted phrase
of John's is "Pure contemplation consists of receiving." This indeed sounds very passive until one exam-
ines it more closely. The Spanish is "*Contemplación
pura consiste en recibir.*" The meaning of *recibir*, however,
is not a completely passive receptivity, but rather a
receiving as one might receive a guest into one's
house. It connotes a welcoming feeling, even a welcoming with open arms. How different the phrase
would sound if it were translated "Pure contemplation consists of welcoming with open arms!"[11]

Another example is even more striking. John speaks
of beginning contemplative experience as characterized by "simple, loving awareness." Again this can
sound very passive. The Spanish here is "*advertencia
amorosa, simple.*" The significant term is *advertencia*, for
which "awareness" is a rather tepid translation. In
modern Spanish usage, *advertencia* means "Attention!"
in the sense of warning or alarm. John himself ex-

plains that *advertencia* is a very dynamic attentiveness. He likens it to the kind of attentiveness one gives to a dearly loved one or the vigilance of standing alert on a watchtower.[12]

If we can refrain from clinging to the either/or dualism of "God and me," we can begin to appreciate the more subtle nuances implied in John and Teresa's use of "active" and "passive." To be sure, there is a distinct feeling of difference between meditation and contemplation, between what we feel we are doing on our own and what seems to come as sheer gift from God. In the more active dimensions of the spiritual life, we have the sense of undertaking practices or disciplines that depend upon our own intentionality and effort. We usually have a certain goal in mind, something we want to achieve by our efforts. We often also have a sense of success or failure.

Then, as the dark night leads us into more contemplative territory, the feeling of autonomous effort gives way to a greater sense of acceptance, of willingness and welcoming. Goals disappear, to be replaced by simple prayers of desire, and success and failure finally lose their meaning entirely. The experience indeed feels more like "letting go and letting God," but our own continuing yes remains active, a dynamic and necessary component of a mysterious relationship that surpasses all understanding.

The Times of the Night

According to John, each dimension of the soul—the outer, sensory aspect and the inner, spiritual aspect—undergoes its own kind of liberation. Thus John divides the dark night of the soul into two basic parts: the dark night of the senses and the dark night of the spirit.

During the dark night of the senses, the soul finds freedom from its attachments to particular sensory gratifications, while the dark night of the spirit releases attachments to rigid beliefs and ways of thinking, frozen memories and expectations, and compulsive, automatic choices. Since the intellect, memory, and will cannot grasp God, they, like the senses, need to be "darkened," emptied of the false gods they cling to. John says the night of the senses is very common and happens to many. The night of the spirit, though, occurs more rarely.[13]

The night of the senses and the night of the spirit are phases of the dark night of the soul. John compares the night of the senses to dusk, when things have just become hazy. The night of the spirit (which he also calls the night of faith) is like midnight, a deeper darkness in which all things are obscured. Although he describes them in this linear fashion, there is no hard-and-fast sequence; they overlap and often happen simultaneously. And there is of course a third part of the night: the coming of the dawn.[14]

John further divides the nights of senses and spirit into active and passive dimensions. I realize that this takes us into increasingly abstract territory, but I think it's important in order to understand John's thinking. Remember that "active" and "passive" are expedient terms reflecting people's sense of whether something seems to result from their own efforts or instead comes as a gift. As we have seen, the real process is much more intimate and mysterious.

The Active Nights

In the active nights, people are aware of participating in their own spiritual journey. They do what they can to intentionally further the process. The *active night of the senses* usually involves spiritual practices such as prayer, meditation, journaling, retreats, and spiritual guidance. In addition, John recommends that one consciously attempt to refrain from any kind of overindulgence. This may take ascetic forms such as fasting, or it may simply be part of healthful living, such as exercise and good nutrition.

The *active night of the spirit* is characterized by similar disciplines and restraints applied to the intellect, memory, will, and imagination. John's primary example here is of practicing the virtues. He says that the three theological virtues (faith, hope, and love) are instrumental in freeing the spirit from its attachments. Faith darkens and empties the intellect, hope frees the memory, and love liberates the will.

For John, the practice of the virtues is not a simple matter of trying to act in faithful, hopeful, and loving ways. Although such attempts may be well intentioned, they can easily reinforce our existing attachments rather than free us from them. A common example is someone's becoming overly scrupulous, even compulsive, in believing and doing all the right things. Since this leads toward greater self-preoccupation rather than freedom for love, John advises moderation. Instead of building more habits of belief and action, John wants the intellect, memory, and will—

which can hold only substitutes for the reality of God—to be gradually *emptied* of all their content. To this end, John advocates a dispassionate attitude toward all insights, concepts, images, and even inspirations, no matter how profound or holy they may seem.[15]

Both of the active nights involve disciplines of restraint, attempts to reverse usual habits of stuffing oneself with sensory, intellectual, spiritual, or any other kind of gratification. Both are movements toward subtraction rather than addition, simplification rather than complication, emptying instead of filling, relinquishment rather than accumulation.

To participate in the active nights, John says it is best to take up one's cross and to imitate Christ to the best of one's ability. This involves not only following Jesus' external behavior, but also his inner attitude of self-emptying and willingness. With Christ as the model, John emphasizes that liberation comes neither through understanding, nor through any perception or image of God, but only through the total emptying of all these things. Only then can the "perfect purity" of love shine through the human soul.[16]

I find it sad that John's description of the active nights is his most well known writing. Outside of

Spain, people are often more familiar with his discussion of spiritual disciplines than with his poetry. "You must deny yourself completely in everything," he says. Excerpts such as the following are common:

> *To achieve satisfaction in everything,*
> *Desire it in nothing.*
> *To possess everything,*
> *Desire to have nothing.*
> *To be everything,*
> *Desire to be nothing.*
> *To know everything,*
> *Desire to know nothing.*[17]

As harsh as such words sound, they have captured people's attention because they suggest something to *do*. Reading these maxims alone, out of context, may even suggest that if we only work hard enough at it, we can control our spiritual destiny. It is this kind of emphasis that has given John his undeserved reputation as an austere, life-denying ascetic; in truth such writings constitute only a small fraction of his work. Both John and Teresa pay relatively little attention to the active aspect of the spiritual life because they know from experience that our own autonomous efforts can accomplish very little. They are much more interested in the passive dimension, the work God does within us, seemingly beyond our own will and intention.

John's most well known ascetical writing, from which the above lines are taken, is found in the thirteenth chapter of the first book of his *Ascent of Mount Carmel.* Less well known is that, in the very next chapter, John says quite bluntly that all this effort does not work. We cannot do it on our own. We cannot even begin the journey without God's instilling "deeper, more urgent longings" within us. And still more grace is needed to find "the courage to be in the darkness of everything." Thus the passive nights come.[18]

The Passive Nights

It is easy to understand that we cannot free ourselves on our own; life itself teaches us that. But it's a lesson many of us seem determined to forget. Even now, with a lifetime of self-improvement failures behind me, I still keep trying. As soon as I become aware of some bad habit or personality defect in myself, I try to take it into my own hands

and fix it *on my own.* It's possible that I have been successful at some of these attempts, but for the life of
me I can't think of an example. I usually have to fail
several times before I admit that I cannot do it alone.
Giving up the striving isn't easy. We human beings
naturally try to achieve satisfaction in all things
through our own autonomous effort and control. This
is just as true in our search for spiritual fulfillment as
it is in the rest of life. We may yearn to "let go and let
God," but it usually doesn't happen until we have
exhausted our own efforts. There is a relentless willfulness in us that seldom ceases until we have been
brought to our knees by incapacity and failure.

In John's vision, it is during the passive nights that
God's grace flows through the ruins of our failed
attempts, softens our willfulness, and takes us where
we could not go on our own. It is also during the passive nights that we feel our own version of the pain
and loss that cause the dark night to be associated
with suffering. And it is during the passive nights that
the real liberation takes place. All the rest has, at best,
been nothing but preparation.

In the *passive night of the senses,* John says, God is
freeing us from the idols we have made of possessions,
relationships, feelings, and behaviors. As always in the

precious process of the night, this divine liberation
takes place in ways that are obscure to us. Sometimes
we may experience it as an inner relaxation and letting go. At other times it may feel like something we
cling to is being ripped away from us. Either way, the
freedom comes only through relinquishment. The
actual experience may feel like delightful liberation or
tragic bereavement, or it may happen so deeply that
we are not aware of it at all. But one thing is certain:
the process of freedom is one of *subtraction*—we are
left more empty than when we began.

Prayer is never really separate from the rest of life,
so the passive night of the senses brings a similar
change in one's spiritual activities. Prayer that used
to be full of consolation and peace may now seem
empty and dry. Worship and other church activities
are not as rewarding as they used to be. It is increasingly difficult to maintain daily "active" practices like
prayer, meditation, journaling, or spiritual reading.
In general, one finds oneself losing interest in the
spiritual things that used to offer so much gratification. Even the images of God one has depended
upon may gradually lose their significance.

All the while, as we have seen, the process happens
in obscurity. We do not understand that the changes

we are experiencing are opening us to more free and complete love. Instead, our most common reaction is self-doubt. Because we assume we should be in charge of our spiritual lives, our first reaction is usually, "What am I doing wrong?" This self-doubt, combined with loss and confusion, explains why the passive night of the senses is often unpleasant, why it involves territory we would not choose to traverse on our own. I want to reiterate, though, that the experience can in some ways be pleasurable. A lessening of dependence on one's work or relationships can sometimes feel freeing. Even the loss of one's habitual spiritual activities—especially if one has been doing them out of habit or obligation—can feel like a burden lifted. Pleasant or unpleasant, however, all such experiences do involve *loss,* and there is always a certain emptiness left behind.

The *passive night of the spirit,* as John sees it, is the process of emptying and freeing the spiritual faculties: intellect, memory, and will. It liberates them from attachment to rigidly held beliefs, understandings, dreams, expectations, and habitual, compulsive ways of loving and behaving righteously. In my experience, the most universal change accomplished by the passive night of the spirit is the blurring of one's belief in being separate from God, from other people, and from the rest of creation. Increasingly, one feels *a part of* all things instead of *apart from* them. Such softenings can happen with any rigidly held habitual beliefs and concepts.

Again, we may experience the relinquishment as a gentle inner relaxation or as a more brutal ripping away of something we hold dear. Perhaps a person has held a religious belief such as "Anyone who isn't Christian is doomed to hell" or "Dancing is sinful." The person may experience a subtle internal easing of such an attitude over time and one day realize it no longer seems true. Or a life situation may dramatically contradict such beliefs. A college friend of mine was a fervent Christian Scientist who continually alienated people with tirades against medical care. Then he fell in love with a wonderful girl who just happened to be a premed student. His "crisis of faith" was agonizing, and he finally broke up with the girl. Afterward, though, he was much less compelled to convince others of his beliefs.

We become attached not only to our beliefs and concepts, but also to our dreams and expectations. An obvious modern example is when one partner in a relationship relentlessly expects the other partner to change abusive behavior. The attachment here is not to the abusive partner, but to an idealized image of what the changed person would be like. Such dreams die hard. And after they finally do die, it may take a long time to appreciate the gift of freedom one has received. As another example, some people grow up believing that their faith and righteousness will bring them health, happiness, and even wealth. Sooner or later, life will likely teach them otherwise. At first they may ask the usual question: "Where did I go wrong?" Later they may be grateful for having developed a more realistic outlook—that the spiritual life is not, finally, a means to achieving one's own superficial desires.

The deeper, more penetrating—and usually more painful—dimensions of the passive night of the spirit have to do with changes in people's habitual sense of relationship with God. A common experience, often confusing but not too painful, is that the word "God" loses its meaning. That word, which used to bring forth familiar images and feelings, now seems inadequate and somehow even wrong. And there seems to be no satisfactory substitute. One learns experientially what John and Teresa continually affirm: no words,

not even the divine names, can ever adequately portray the Reality.

A much more unsettling experience is the loss of
the sense of God's presence, which can often feel like
being abandoned by God. Many people are used to a
consistent and long-lasting feeling of the presence of
God in their lives. It may be a distinct sense of presence, of companionship everywhere. It may happen
more in relationship with children, spouse, or other
beloved people. It may occur in special places, as in
church or outdoors in nature. Even more often it is
just too subtle to describe at all. Whatever form it
takes, however, it is sensible, palpable, and deeply
meaningful. Then, sometimes, it disappears.

Though we don't realize it at the time, when habitual senses of God do disappear in the process of the
dark night, it is surely because it is time for us to relinquish our attachment to them. We have made an idol
our images and feelings of God, giving them more
importance than the true God they represent. This
can happen with any image or sense of the Divine.
For example, some people have a long-lasting sense
of God as distant, harsh, and judgmental. Others feel
that God absolutely controls their destiny; they have

nothing to say about it. Others feel much the opposite: that if there is any God at all, it is a God who
leaves them alone to fend for themselves. Still others
carry with them a steady sense of God's loving presence, comfortable and reassuring but static, never
inviting challenges or risks. No matter what specific
form they may take, all such rigidly held feelings
about God restrict our openness to the incomprehensible divine reality.

The passive night of the spirit serves to loosen
our hold on such expectations, to leave us more willing to accept God's being as God will. As with other
changes occurring in the dark night, this process can
sometimes feel delightfully liberating; bright new
vistas of possibility open as we let go of old habits.
More often, though, it feels as though the foundations
of faith are being shaken. It is easy to understand
how devastating such an experience might be. For
people who are deeply in love with God, the loss of
a habitual sense of God's presence can seem like a
greater abandonment than the loss of human love.
Here again, people are likely to feel it is somehow
their fault; they wonder where they went so wrong to
cause the divine Lover to disappear. And when this
loss is accompanied by lassitude and emptiness in

prayer and other spiritual practices and lack of motivation for them, a person may easily wonder, "Do I even believe in anything anymore? Do I even care?"

When the spiritual life feels so uprooted, it can be almost impossible to believe—or even to consider—that what's really going on is a graceful process of liberation, a letting go of old, limiting habits to make room for fresh openness to love. Still, I have known some people who carried at least a glimpse of this wisdom through their experience. One said, "I guess it's time for me to abide in faith." Another simply said, "God's weaning me." These people never grieved or raged about what had happened. They acknowledged that it was a loss, but they seemed somehow to know that what they had lost was not God, only their palpable feeling of God.

Therein lies the wisdom. Teresa and John both say that we easily become so attached to feelings *of* and *about* God that we equate them *with* God. We forget that these sensations are only speaking to us of the divine One. They are only messengers. Instead, we take them for the whole of God's self, and thus we wind up worshiping our own feelings. This is perhaps the most common idolatry of the spiritual life.

I remember having an almost continual sense of God's presence as a very small child. The feeling receded as I grew older and other things occupied my attention. Later in life, when I embarked on my intentional "spiritual journey," I realized how much I had missed that feeling of continual companionship. I sought to recover it in prayer and meditation, and I prayed for it to return. I experienced the Holy through other people, through nature, and in many other mediated ways. But what I longed for was that old nonmediated, *im*mediate sense of direct, palpable relationship. I searched and prayed for it for nearly twenty-five years. Then, when I was very sick as a result of cancer chemotherapy, it came back to me. And since then, that sense of presence has never left me. I can feel it anywhere, anytime. All I have to do is turn my attention toward it. I love it and surely would hate to lose it. It's the answer to a very long prayer. But I know it is not God. It is only a sense *of* God. I don't think I make an idol of it, so I don't imagine it will need to be taken away. If at some point I do lose it again, I hope I will be given the wisdom to continue to trust God in the absence of any sense of God.

Transformation

I want to say again that the times of the night do not happen in a linear, step-by-step progression. John portrays them that way for clarity, but in real life they overlap, intermingle, and even, as Teresa emphasized, "often return to the beginning."[19]

Thus the night of the spirit does not wait until the night of the senses is over—if it did, it would probably never happen! Similarly, the passive nights do not wait until the active nights are finished. To some extent, we can assume that various dimensions of the night are *always* going on in our lives. God is always working obscurely within us. And, even more mysteriously, some part of us is saying yes to God's invitations to go where we do not want to go.

Viewed in this way, the dark night of the soul is not an event one passes through and gets beyond, but rather a deep ongoing process that characterizes our spiritual life. In this sense, the dark night *is* a person's hidden life with God. John takes this even further, saying that the night is not just the activity of God; it *is* God. "This dark night," he says, "is an inflow of God into the soul."[20]

Constance FitzGerald, a contemporary Carmelite authority on John's theology, points out John's assertion that this divine inflow is the "loving Wisdom of God." Specifically, she says, it is the active presence of Jesus Christ as Wisdom, as divine Sophia. Thus, "Dark night is not primarily *some thing,* an impersonal darkness like a difficult situation or distressful psychological condition, but *someone,* a presence leaving an indelible imprint on the human spirit and consequently on one's entire life."[21]

In the obscurity of the night, we may not recognize that imprint or the presence that makes it. But as we become freer, we have more glimpses of the dawn, more awareness of these deeper currents of our lives. And even then the mystery remains. John emphasizes that even in moments of great clarity there is still a place in our "deepest center" where the Holy One dwells "in secret and alone," a hidden place "where neither the devil nor the intellect" can interfere.[22]

And the intellect is indeed capable of interfering. So many times I have become aware of some subtlety of my spiritual life, some experience or insight, only to watch my mind grab for it and try to make something of it. Until one learns or is given the contemplative capacity to be aware of a thing without having to meddle with it, it is necessary for the most precious things to remain hidden.

Still, we do experience intermittent glimpses or reflections of the deep spiritual currents flowing within us. From time to time we might become aware of our desire for God, our longing for goodness, truth, and beauty. We might feel relief or grief from letting go of some attachment. Maybe we are momentarily overwhelmed with simple gratitude for this life we are given. But these experiences are only waves on the surface, mere hints of the deep currents of our souls moving far beneath our consciousness.

In this sense, I think we can consider reshaping what it might mean when one says one has gone through a dark night of the soul. From the individual's perspective, dark night may simply refer to an experience of loss and desolation. Sometimes that's all it means: a difficult time in one's life. There is no recognition of grace or liberation, and if gratitude is felt, it is simply for having survived. At other times, there is a strong sense that the experience, however pleasant or unpleasant, was a vehicle for gifts of grace: self-knowledge perhaps, a sense of closeness to God, or deepened faith and trust. Then there may be thanksgiving for having had the experience, even though one might never want to repeat it. Like many people, I feel this way about my experience with cancer and chemotherapy. I wouldn't have missed it for the world, but I certainly would never want to go through it again.

Summary

My emphasis here has been on how the dark night liberates desire by diminishing attachment. The immediate result is expansion of human freedom. Freedom, however, is not an end in itself. It is not just freedom *from* something; it must also be freedom *for* something. In the spiritual life, freedom is for nothing other than love. Human beings exist because of love, and the meaning and goal of our lives is love. In Christian understanding, everything that is authentic in the spiritual life points toward the increasing fulfillment of the two great commandments: to love God and other people in a completely unfettered way. Liberation from attachment is only a means to this end.

To experience the pinnacle of the journey, the dawn after the night, is to realize the union with God that has always existed. John says this realization of union *is* the fullness of love—so much so that the person's desire is indistinguishable from God's desire. Now, with "great conformity" between the sensory and spiritual dimensions of the soul, John says to God, "I want what you want, and what you do not want, I do not want, nor could I, nor would it even enter my mind."[23]

Along the way toward freedom and realization, many other changes are taking place. Desire itself becomes transformed. The twelfth-century abbot and spiritual writer St. Bernard of Clairvaux explains one way in which this happens. We usually begin, he says, by seeking gratification and fulfillment through our own devices. He calls this the "love of self for one's own sake." When life teaches us that this doesn't work, we often turn to God, a higher power, and seek the consolations that are given through grace. In Bernard's words, this is the "love of God for one's own sake." Gradually, we find ourselves falling in love not with the consolations of God, but with the God who gives the consolations: the "love of God for

God's sake." In the atmosphere of this love, Bernard says we finally begin to discover how lovable we ourselves are: "love of self for God's sake.[24]

Another development, which Teresa especially emphasizes, is in the area of self-knowledge. One sees one's own true nature with increasing clarity. In the beginning of each cycle of experiencing the night, self-knowledge often comes painfully as we confront our pettiness and selfishness. But as Bernard predicted, each time we approach the dawn, when the realization of union deepens and we begin to glimpse ourselves through God's eyes, we recognize more of our inherent goodness and beauty. Teresa says, "I can find nothing with which to compare the great beauty of a soul . . . we can hardly form any conception of the soul's great dignity and beauty." And John, trying to describe the experience of the soul in realized union, says, "The soul sees herself as a queen."[25]

Throughout every aspect of the journey through the night, there is a gradual easing of the feeling of autonomous effort, the white-knuckled striving that seeks to control and manage everything. In place of the striving, one finds a growing willingness, an increasing *receptivity* in the sense of welcoming with open arms. This is nowhere so obvious as in prayer, as the work of meditation eases and the flowing openness of contemplation takes its place.

When Teresa, John, and other spiritual writers use the word "contemplation," they are referring to something very different from the popular secular meanings of thinking, planning, or examining. In the context of prayer, contemplation always has a sacred quality as a sheer gift of grace. The word comes from Latin roots *com* and *templum,* "with" and "temple." With every step from meditation into contemplation, one finds oneself standing on truly sacred ground.

CHAPTER FOUR

WITH A TEMPLE

Meditation and Contemplation

Prayer is the soul's sincere desire
Uttered or unexpressed;
The motion of a hidden fire,
That trembles in the breast.

—*James Montgomery*[1]

Most of the transformation we have been discussing thus far takes place in life as a whole.
The process of the dark night eases the restraints our
attachments place on us, enabling us to live more fully
and lovingly. It deepens our trust in God's presence
and in the essential goodness of life and of ourselves.
It leaves us emptier—knowing less and having less

than when we started—and this emptiness makes us freer than we would ever have dared to expect.

As these changes take place in life as a whole, similar transformations occur in the experience of prayer. It is to this more interior dimension that Teresa and John dedicate most of their teaching.

Experiences of Prayer

Both John and Teresa offer rich insights into the transitions between meditation and contemplation, but I think Teresa's are more approachable. Unlike John, she frequently refers to her own personal experience, which makes it much easier to identify with her. And although Teresa does her best to be abstract and analytical, she is never as successful at it as John. This keeps her descriptions more earthy and practical. For these reasons, I will focus primarily on Teresa's descriptions of prayer experiences. I will return to John's thinking in the next chapter's discussion of signs and spirits.

As John divides the dark nights of senses and spirit into active and passive dimensions, so Teresa divides prayer into active and passive categories. Remember the subtleties of this distinction—it's not as simple as "I do it" or "God does it." A good way of understanding Teresa's description is that active prayer is characterized by what feels like personal effort inspired and empowered by God's grace, while passive prayer feels like God's work welcomed by personal willingness.

Teresa says there are two basic kinds of active prayer. *Vocal prayer* is simple rote recitation: going through the motions of saying prayers without really appreciating what one is doing. As soon as one becomes mindful of the act of praying, however, vocal prayer becomes *mental prayer.* The difference is simple awareness.[2]

Active mental prayer, for Teresa, is essentially synonymous with *meditation.* She describes three kinds of meditation. The first is *reflection,* in which one uses one's faculties to think about or visualize some aspect of the spiritual life. The second kind of meditation is *active recollection.* Here a person's effort is directed more toward awareness itself, toward a simple attentiveness to the divine presence. Many of today's popular meditation practices such as Centering prayer, Transcendental Meditation, Christian Meditation, Zen, and Vipassana belong to this category.[3]

The third kind of meditation, which Teresa calls *passive recollection,* marks the first step toward contemplation in prayer. During the practice of meditation one begins to experience moments of open, immediate awareness that occur effortlessly—and that seem simply to be given. Teresa says that when attention drifts off or away somewhere, God seems to call it back "like a good shepherd with a whistle so gentle [the soul] almost fails to hear it." For Teresa, this kind of experience heralds the transition between *mental* prayer and *quiet* prayer, between *active* prayer and *passive* prayer, and between *meditation* and *contemplation.*[4]

Meditation and Contemplation

Christian mysticism has traditionally made a very clear distinction between meditation and contemplation. Put simply, meditation is what we seem to be able to do and accomplish on our own, while contemplation is what seems to come as sheer gift. To use John's words, meditation includes all the "acts and exercises" of prayer and spiritual practice—the things one does intentionally.[5]

In contrast, contemplation cannot be practiced. Although it is common today to speak of "practicing" contemplative prayer, Teresa and John would see this as referring to simple and quiet forms of meditation, not to contemplative prayer itself. For them, contemplation is entirely God's gift of grace. There is no way to make it happen. It cannot be achieved or acquired. It happens when it happens, and all we can do is be willing, say yes to it, welcome it. Because it is so clearly a divine gift, contemplation is especially sacred in the mystical tradition. This is reflected in the Latin origins of the word: *com templum,* "with a temple."

The distinction between meditation and contemplation is critical to understanding Teresa's and John's view of the spiritual life. In their day, meditation normally meant using one's faculties (intellect, memory, will, and imagination) to reflect upon scripture and the life of Christ. In a larger sense, meditation applies to all intentional prayer and spiritual practices. It can take any number of forms: from delving into scripture to repeating a holy word, from journaling to liturgical dancing, from inward visualization to simply going through the day with mindfulness. But whatever its form, meditation is always something we feel we are choosing to do, something that requires our intentionality.

For Teresa and John, contemplation has no roots in human intent or effort except for the deep and secret welcoming, the yes that we often don't even know we're saying. Apart from this hidden willingness, contemplation is completely independent of human will and the rest of the faculties as well. We may desire it, pray for it, and imagine what it might be like, but we can neither understand it nor make it happen.

Contemplation has been defined in many ways over the centuries, but except for one notable distortion it has always been seen as coming as a sheer gift, given in God's own way and in God's own time. The exception is the idea of *acquired* or *achieved* contemplation, which is traceable to a compiler of John's works, Tomás de Jesus, some of whose writings were mistaken for John's own.[6]

Classical descriptions of contemplation frequently include two psychological qualities. First, awareness is *open,* not focused on one thing to the exclusion of others. In meditation, as in most of our usual endeavors, we put a certain amount of effort into focusing attention, often struggling to exclude what we would

call "distractions." In contemplation, this effortful
focusing disappears and awareness assumes an open,
all-embracing, panoramic quality. In contemplation,
then, one is simply present to what is—nothing is shut
out, nothing excluded. There can be no distractions
in contemplation because everything is simply a part
of what is going on. The twelfth-century theologian
Hugh of St. Victor described contemplation as "the
alertness of the understanding which, finding everything plain, grasps it clearly with entire apprehension."
This "finding everything plain" implies an unfocused
openness in which nothing captures attention because
nothing is special or everything is equally special. To
use Teresa's words, "The Presence, whom the soul
has at its side, makes it attentive to everything."[7]

The second psychological quality commonly associated with contemplation is its *centeredness in the present
moment.* This is the "timeless moment" of the mystics,
the "eternal now"—what the twentieth-century
Quaker educator Thomas Kelly called "continuously
renewed immediacy."[8]

These two psychological qualities coexist naturally.
If contemplation is characterized by open, unfocused
presence to what *is,* then it is always going to be *in the
now.* It is important to understand the nature of this

present-centeredness. It does not mean, for example, that thoughts of the future or memories of the past are necessarily absent. Memories and future planning can happen as they usually do, but without kidnapping one's attention away from whatever else is going on at the time. Instead, they are experienced as *part of* what is occurring in the moment. Thus one might be sitting under a tree, aware of all one's surroundings, feeling the breeze, hearing a bird singing, seeing clouds passing in the sky. A memory of the past or a thought of the future comes along, and it is simply another event happening in the moment, perhaps passing in the same way as the clouds.

This open, present-centered awareness is something we all have experienced, at least for short periods of time. Normally, however, our awareness soon becomes captivated by one thing or another, and we find ourselves quickly returned to our usual focused attention. If we remember the moment at all, we may look back on it with a kind of poignant longing. Thomas Kelly put it well, I think, in his wish to the moment: "Stay, thou art so sweet."[9]

I have used the term "psychological" to describe the openness and immediacy of contemplation because they are governed by how the nervous system

mediates attention. To some extent, the openness and
present-centeredness of awareness can be practiced
and developed. Many meditation methods aim in this
direction. An example is the simple practice of attending to one's breathing. The attempt is to notice
every aspect of the breath without controlling or
influencing it. Over time, this and similar practices
can lead to the capacity to choose an openness and
immediacy of awareness almost at will.

But these psychological qualities are not all there is
to contemplation. The one essential quality of contemplation that all the mystics affirm, and that *must*
come as sheer gift, is love. Immediacy and openness
of awareness may rise and fall, but one unwavering
constant remains: *contemplation is loving.* And this love
can neither be practiced nor achieved. We can, and
certainly should, try to act in loving ways. All religions
advocate this. But the way we act lovingly is often
determined by our attachments. It is self-originated
and unfree. We encounter true, unattached love only
by falling into it or waking up to discover it, often
being surprised by it. Much as we might long for it,
we cannot make it happen. The freely loving quality
of contemplation must be kindled, prompted, drawn
forth, or, if you will, infused within us by God. Teresa

speaks of the soul as a sobbing child: "So this child must be hushed with a loving caress which will move it to a gentle love." In John's words, "The soul moves on, enkindled with yearnings of purest love for God, without knowing where they come from or upon what they are based."[10]

It is this mystical loving quality that makes contemplation so clearly sacred, holy ground, "with a temple." It is also the reason that no matter what we say about it, contemplation finally defies description. Again and again, John speaks of contemplation itself as being "dark." One does not know, in the usual sense, what one is experiencing. The experience—if it even *is* an experience—is beyond all words and comprehension.[11]

The Interior Garden

Because contemplation so defies objective descriptions, Teresa and John rely on metaphor to convey its mysteries. In so doing, they have created some of the most compelling imagery of mystical literature. One of Teresa's most well known metaphors is that of the interior garden, by which she very effectively portrays the differences between meditation and contemplation. We find it in her first book, her *Life*, written several years before she met John.[12]

Teresa likens the human soul to a garden, with God dwelling in the center. The garden contains many exquisite flowers, which she says are the virtues. It is only natural, Teresa says, that we would want our soul-garden to be beautifully cultivated and fragrant so that God will take "delight among these virtues."

As we have seen, John also speaks of cultivating virtues as part of his recommendations for the active night of the spirit. Teresa's recipe, however, is far less complicated. She says the beginning soul-gardener need not worry about tilling the ground, planting seeds, or even uprooting weeds, because God has already done all these things "by the time a soul is determined to practice prayer."

These are radical assumptions, even in our day. Teresa is saying we do not need to instill virtues in ourselves, for God has already planted them within us. Nor do we need to worry about unwanted weeds in the garden; that too is God's work. She even implies that too much concern over virtues and vices may distract us from our primary task in tending the garden, which is only to see that the garden receives sufficient water. For Teresa, the water is nothing other than prayer, and prayer is nothing other than loving attentiveness.

Watering the soul-garden with prayer may seem simple, but Teresa knows it is often not easy. She describes four ways the watering can happen, representing four degrees, or "grades," of prayer ("*grados de oración*"). The first degree is meditation; the other three are deepening dimensions of contemplation in which the person's sense of autonomous effort in prayer is increasingly replaced by a feeling of God's deep and obscure divine activity.

The first way of watering the garden is by hauling the water from a well in a bucket. This is meditation, and Teresa says it is a "great labor" that provides very little water. Still, it helps the virtues sprout. The second way is by means of a waterwheel, which is "less work and gives more water." This is the prayer of quiet, the beginning of contemplation, and it brings the virtues to bud. In the third way, a nearby stream or spring does most of the watering naturally. This "saturates the ground more completely," and the gardener needs only to supplement it occasionally. This third prayer brings the virtues to flower. In the fourth way, rain waters the garden. This is the prayer of union, where there is no effort on the person's part at all, and the virtues bear fruit.

As was the custom in her time, Teresa's description of these four degrees sounds like a direct progression from meditation through contemplation to the prayer of union. This makes it all too easy to assume a stepwise advancement from one stage to the next. As with John's stages of the night, though, Teresa's degrees of prayer are not to be understood as occurring in a strictly linear way. They continually overlap and recur in cycles. What Teresa and John have done is unraveled the varied experiences people have in prayer and portrayed them in ways they hope will be coherent and understandable. They present them in a logical, even hierarchical order for clarity, not because they necessarily occur that way.

Further, these degrees of prayer are not steady states, but rather *experiences* that happen intermittently in prayer. The different kinds of prayer experiences mix with one another. People experience moments of contemplation in the very beginning, though these are usually short-lived and often go unrecognized. Similarly, when a person is experiencing an abundance of contemplation, there are still occasions for returning to meditation. Over time, however, as people experience and recognize contemplation more often, they naturally spend less time and effort in meditation. With this background, we can look at Teresa's four experiences of prayer in more detail.

The Well and the Bucket: Meditation

The first way of prayer, the drawing of the bucket from the well, is *meditation*. The work of meditation involves using the faculties and dealing with distractions ("keeping the senses recollected"). Teresa was very flexible about the form meditation could take. It might be reflecting on scripture passages or imagining events in the life of Jesus. Or it might involve looking at works of art or scenes in nature. She herself advocated a gentle practice of the presence of God very like the one Brother Lawrence popularized a century later. This was a simple attempt to remember God's presence in all that she did. She also described trying to create an internal imaginary picture of Christ. Overall, she said people should practice whatever works best, "whatever is most helpful."[13]

When one feels as if everything relies upon one's own effort, even the simplest ways of attentiveness in meditation can take a lot of energy. Teresa says one may become so tired drawing the water from the well that one can "no longer move one's arms." And often the well seems dry; the meditation yields little or no gratification (consolation). But the work must go on regardless, because it is "all we can do." Teresa says the work is its own reward because it is a labor of love. It is a way of taking up one's cross, an expression of one's desire for God, and God deeply appreciates it. It is our prayer in action, the only way "we can make progress on our own, of course with the help of God."[14]

Consolations, the good feelings of prayer, come in meditation during moments that Teresa calls *active recollection*. These are times when the work of meditation quiets the mind and brings one's awareness into the immediate moment. The content of the consolation varies; one may experience deep stillness and peace, be overcome by gratitude or beauty, or be moved to tears by powerful emotion. Whatever the content, the experience is delightful, and it always encourages one's desire for God.

Teresa uses the word *contentos* for these consolations that occur in meditation. She says that because such experiences seem partly due to our own efforts, we are "quite right to feel satisfaction at having worked in such a way." But she immediately points out that we cannot take all the credit—without God's grace such good feelings would be impossible. She also emphasizes that the *contentos* of meditation are like other good feelings that happen naturally in normal life, as when one is reunited with a loved one or is successful in a difficult business undertaking. Thus the *contentos* of meditation have a physical quality. Teresa says they arise within a person's senses, and the pleasure they cause encourages the person's prayer.[15]

The Waterwheel: The Prayer of Quiet

At unpredictable times, one experiences the second way of watering the garden, by means of a waterwheel. Teresa envisions a hand crank turning the wheel, which feeds water into an aqueduct that carries the water to the garden. Here, she says, there is much less effort, and far more water is produced. The prayer of quiet is characterized by what Teresa calls *passive recollection*, which is a first taste of contemplative experience. Now, instead of working and concentrating, "the faculties are recollected within the soul, so that its delight may be even greater."[16]

This glimpse of contemplative experience brings a different kind of consolation, which Teresa calls *gustos*. Teresa explains that the *contentos* of meditation "arise in human nature and are directed toward God," while the *gustos* of contemplation "arise in God, but human nature feels and enjoys them."[17]

Thus the *gustos* of contemplation are God's own delight, overflowing into the person's senses. These feelings have a supernatural quality, a hint of ultimate satisfaction. "The soul is now rising above its miseries," Teresa says, "and is receiving a taste of the delights of glory. . . . This quietness and recollection makes itself clearly felt through the satisfaction and peace which it brings to the soul, together with a very great calm, joy and sweet delight in the faculties."[18]

As blissful as the *gustos* of contemplation may be, the shift away from meditation is usually confusing and often experienced as unpleasant. In fact, the prayer of quiet is frequently preceded by a profound absence of *contentos*. If one looks for prayer experiences of the dark night of the soul in Teresa's writing, they begin here, as meditation eases as if to make room for the prayer of quiet to happen on its own. In this place, she says, one may "experience nothing but dryness, dislike and distaste." The transition is dark, obscure; the person does not understand what is happening. "When the Lord begins to grant these favors, the soul itself does not understand them, or know what it ought to do . . . and its trial may be heavy." She says she herself "endured these trials for many years," during which time she was grateful to get even "one drop of water from this blessed well."[19]

No one, Teresa says, can predict when or how the moments of passive recollection and their consoling *gustos* will happen. Only God knows. "It is not a question of our will. . . . It happens only when God is pleased to grant it. . . . However much we practice meditation, no matter how we force ourselves and no matter how many tears we shed, we cannot produce this water. . . . It is given only to whom God wills to give it and often when the soul is not thinking of it at all." Teresa cautions people not to try to hurry things up by stilling the mind to create a contrived state of recollection. Such attempts are likely to backfire. "To keep the soul's faculties busy and at the same time keep them quiet is foolishness," she says. "The very effort the soul makes to try to stop thinking may awaken thought and cause it to think a great deal."[20]

Teresa foresees the natural question her readers will have. "But how, you will ask, are we to gain these favors if we do not strive for them?" Her response is unequivocal: *relinquish all attempts to achieve more advanced states of prayer.* "We should not try to lift up our spirits until they are lifted up by the Lord." Instead, she says, we should stay with our simple labor of love. "The important thing is not to think much, but to love much. Therefore, do whatever most arouses you to love."[21]

When the prayer of quiet and passive recollection do happen, the experience is so sweet, the *gustos* so delicate, that one wants to remain completely still. It feels as though the slightest movement of mind or body will destroy the experience. Teresa uses two scripture passages to describe how it feels. Referring to the account of the transfiguration (Matt. 17:4), she says the soul feels it has seen the ultimate glory and "wants to build its dwelling there." And she refers to the Mary and Martha story (Luke 10:38–42), saying the soul "enjoys the holy idleness of Mary."[22]

The Stream or Spring:
The "Sleep of the Faculties"

The precious sense of delicacy that characterizes the prayer of quiet seems to relax in the third way of watering the garden, in which the water flows from a nearby stream or spring. God now seems to be doing "practically everything" regarding prayer, and one no longer clings so much to stillness. Teresa says this allows a person to be both Martha and Mary at the same time. It is a feeling of being in the world, but not of it. People go about their normal activities: reading, writing, and engaging in "works of charity" and "affairs of business." All the while, however, there is a certainty that one's "best part is elsewhere." Attention is open and unfocused, yet one is very responsive to the needs of whatever situation one finds oneself in. Teresa says the experience is like listening to two people at once. "We cannot be wholly absorbed in either conversation."[23]

Teresa's use of the term "sleep of the faculties" (sueño de las potencias) is troublesome here—or at least I found it so—because she makes it so clear that the faculties actually function even better than before.

Most of the confusion, I'm convinced, comes from Teresa's attempt to fit her personal experience into categories described in mystical theology texts she had read. It was not until I focused on her description of the *experience,* instead of her terminology, that this third kind of prayer began to make sense to me.[24]

To clarify, Teresa sees all these different experiences of prayer as reflecting the degree to which a person's intellect, memory, and will are "united with God" at a given time. One could also speak of the degree of *absence* of independent, separate, or autonomous feelings. She explains that in the previous stage of prayer, in passive recollection, only the will is united with God in this way. The intellect and memory are not wholly taken over. In the present stage, the faculties are "almost completely united with God, but not so absorbed that they cannot act." And in the stage to come, the prayer of union, all the faculties will be completely united with God.[25]

She then tries to describe what people actually experience in these times when the garden is watered by a stream or spring. The *gustos* are now "incomparably greater" than in the prayer of quiet; their joy is almost unbearably sweet. During these moments, Teresa says, people no longer desire satisfaction from their own senses or accomplishments. But neither are they completely content. More and more, they long simply to be with God. The ache of this yearning for God mixes with the delight of the *gustos* to create a "glorious foolishness, a heavenly insanity." One "does not know whether to speak or be silent, to laugh or to cry." Teresa calls this prayer a "light and heavy cross; light because it is so sweet, yet heavy because at times it is almost too much to bear." One may easily long for death at times like this, seeing it as the only way to satisfy one's yearning for God. But all one can do is "abandon oneself completely into God's arms."[26]

The Rain: The Prayer of Union

Understandably, Teresa is most at a loss in trying to describe the fourth degree of prayer, the "heavenly rain that saturates the whole garden in abundance." She uses the term "union" from the mystical theology she has read, but says she does not know how to explain what this union is or how it happens. In a passage that sounds like modern holistic thought, she goes on to say, "And I can't understand what the mind is, or how it differs from soul or spirit. They all seem the same to me." She is even bewildered in trying to express her gratitude for the "great favors" of this prayer. "Sometimes," she says, "I find it helpful to speak nonsense."[27]

She does better at describing some of the things people experience in this prayer. It often comes when one least expects it. One may feel as if one is swooning, fading away in great delight, or losing touch with body, breathing, and senses. Although one continues to see and hear and feel what is going on around oneself, there is no understanding of these perceptions. Speech is usually impossible.

These rather dramatic experiences of union last only a short time. Teresa says she thinks they never lasted "as long as half an hour" for her. Before one begins a life of conscious prayer, such experiences happen so quickly one completely fails to recognize them. Later, with somewhat more awareness, all one knows is that something quite wonderful has happened. Even later, with more experience and appreciation, they are still short-lived. It never takes long before the intellect or memory becomes active and "begins to be troublesome" again. Teresa explains that this prayer often consists of a to-and-fro experience: the intellect and memory become active while the will remains lovingly given to God. Then God calls the intellect and memory back into quiet suspension, "gathering them back" to join the will in God for a short while. Then they become active again. Over time, however, a deeper, steadier sense of unity grows. Less dramatic and far more ordinary, this lasting "participation" in God can be present in and through all life's activities like a gentle murmur of love.

Struggling to describe what happens to the soul in the more dramatic experiences of the prayer of union, Teresa turns to her own prayer and hears God say, "The soul lets go of everything, daughter, so that it may remain more completely in me. The soul itself no longer lives, but I." God tells her that there is a special kind of knowing that happens in this experience, an "understanding by not understanding."[28]

Teresa does her best to develop this thought, but stumbles wonderfully over herself and winds up admitting defeat: "The will must be completely occupied in loving, but it does not understand how it loves. The understanding, if it does understand, does not understand how it understands. Or at least it cannot comprehend anything of what it understands. It doesn't seem to me that it does understand, because, as I say, it does not understand itself. Nor can I understand this myself!"[29]

The Process

I have taken pains to emphasize that the degrees or kinds of prayer Teresa and John describe are not steady states and that they do not necessarily occur in a stepwise progression. They are, instead, experiences that people encounter at different times in the course of prayer. As I have said, someone just beginning a practice of prayer or meditation will experience moments of realized union, just as people who have given their lives to prayer will sometimes return to effortful meditation.

The spiritual life, however, does not consist of spinning one's wheels. There is a real process taking place, a movement that is definitely heading somewhere. In the beginning, most people are so in the habit of taking charge and being in control that the only possibility for prayer is effortful meditation. For many of us, this is a powerful attachment, if not an outright addiction. The only thing we know is the cultural imperative to take charge of our lives and work toward our goals, so we have no choice but to approach prayer in the same manner.

But hidden deep in all our hearts, I am certain, there is a memory and a longing for simple presence and just being. In large part, this may be what prompts us toward a conscious spiritual life in the first place. But most of us are in bondage to the attitude that passivity, inaction, and surrender hold only negative consequences. Our minds are likely to panic if we try to force ourselves to cease making effort and just be, to "let go and let God." We are likely to feel lazy, irresponsible, and out of control. Thus although meditation may indeed be a lot of work, it is often the only thing that feels comfortable.

This condition of attachment to accomplishment does not prevent experiences of deep quiet or even of union from happening, but it often keeps us from recognizing such moments when they do occur. And even when we notice them—even when we fall in love with them—we find it impossible to bear them for long. Not only do these moments make us feel too passive; they also seem too good to be true. It is very difficult to trust them.

Thus the people whom Teresa and John call "beginners" are likely to find themselves in lovers' quarrels with their own souls. On the one hand, they deeply desire to relinquish their efforts and relax into simple loving presence. On the other, they find such apparent passivity abhorrent and are deeply afraid of the vulnerability and loss of control it requires. Depending upon which feeling is uppermost at the time, people may find themselves either grasping to hold on to a recognized moment of contemplation (which of course seems to destroy it) or running away from it as fast as possible.

Not everyone begins in this way. Teresa acknowledges that there are people who fall into contemplation very naturally, without any apparent interior strife, but they have their own difficulties to face. They have to contend with feeling different from others, at odds with the cultural norm. They often doubt the validity of their natural prayer because it seems so unlike what they have been taught as the "right" way to pray. I have known many people who find it easy and natural to be in the open, willing simplicity of contemplative presence. But they think there's something wrong with them because they see others working so hard at prayer and meditation, and they read all the books that tell people how to "do" it. These people must struggle, as Teresa herself did—and as Brother Lawrence did a century later— to find the personal courage to claim and value their own way.

Thus people are very different in terms of the attachments they bring to the spiritual life. Some begin in severe bondage and choicelessness, while others may be plagued with self-doubt. The prayer journey is seldom if ever completely easy. But Teresa and John both say that God deals with each soul with "esteeming love," addressing each of us with profound respect for who we are and what we need and can bear. And though the process of this soul journey cannot be rigidly categorized into stepwise stages, it *is* a process, and it *is* going somewhere.

Whatever form it takes, the movement of the soul and God is always finding its way toward freedom. In prayer as in the rest of life, it is a movement toward freedom from willfulness, from the compulsion to be in charge and the fear of loss of control. It is a movement toward freedom from "functional atheism," the conviction that effortful autonomous accomplishment is the only hope. And it is a movement toward freedom *for* simple loving presence and appreciation, a willingness to respond and participate in the divine Spirit in the world, a trusting confidence that allows radically loving action.

As one gains experience in the spiritual life, one not only recognizes moments of contemplation and union more readily, but one is also able to bear them and enjoy them more fully in the relative absence of fear or clinging. What is going on is a kind of *deconditioning*, in which the choiceless bondage to habitual patterns is being replaced by free-flowing availability and responsiveness to the real situations of life. This is precisely the transition from meditation to contemplation, and it happens in prayer just as in every other aspect of life.

There are no clear beginning or end points in this process of liberation. Just as no one is completely noncontemplative at the beginning, no one is perfectly contemplative at the end. Yet the growing, deepening process goes on, always toward more and more contemplative living. To my mind, this is all part of the ongoing process of the dark night of the soul. And it will happen in unique ways for each person. Teresa says it took her over two decades to come to even some degree of comfort with her own contemplative prayer. She says she knew someone else for whom it took only a few days.

Regardless of when and how it happens, the dark night of the soul is the transition from bondage to freedom in prayer and in every other aspect of life. In prayer, the movement is from the personal control and effort that characterize meditation to the willingness and simple being that characterize contemplation. As one becomes less willful and controlling in prayer, so one also grows in willingness and trust in the rest of life.

The process just keeps going on. As far as I can tell, the dark night of the soul is endless. This is, for me, the most hopeful thing about it; *the dark night is nothing other than our ongoing relationship with the Divine.* As such, it must always remain mysterious, dark to our understanding and comprehension, illuminated only by brief moments of dawning light. And as such it never ends; it just keeps deepening, revealing more and more intimate layers of freedom for love.

As our dark nights deepen, we find ourselves recovering our love of mystery. When we were children, most of us were good friends with mystery. The world was full of it and we loved it. Then as we grew older, we slowly accepted the indoctrination that mystery exists only to be solved. For many of us, mystery became an adversary; unknowing became a weakness. The contemplative spiritual life is an ongoing reversal of this adjustment. It is a slow and sometimes painful process of becoming "as little children" again, in which we first make friends with mystery and finally fall in love again with it. And in that love we find an ever increasing freedom to *be* who we really are in an identity that is continually emerging and never defined. We are freed to join the dance of life in fullness without having a clue about what the steps are.

The darkness, the holy unknowing that characterizes this freedom, is the opposite of confusion and ignorance. Confusion happens when mystery is an enemy and we feel we must solve it to master our destinies. And ignorance is not knowing that we do not know. In the liberation of the night, we are freed from having to figure things out, and we find delight in knowing that we do not know.

Probably the greatest paradox of the dark night is that since it is so obscure and mysterious, there is no way to positively identify it for ourselves. We may intellectually assume that the mysteries inherent in our lives are evidence of an ongoing dark night. And we may try to believe that experiences of confusion, loss, or relinquishment are part of the night's liberating process. But there is no way to be sure. We may want to believe that a painful experience has meaning and is somehow leading us to greater freedom, but our mind is likely to tell us it happened only because we made some mistake, did something wrong. Ironically, this is most likely to happen if what we are going through really *is* an experience of the dark night of the soul.

Teresa and John deeply understood the paradox. They counseled that we cannot depend upon our own individual knowledge or discernment to determine the nature of our experience. Nor can we depend with certainty upon the counsels of others. In the last analysis, we must simply and radically trust in God's abiding goodness. Still, this did not stop Teresa and John from trying to help. Both of them were all too aware of the hurtful effects of well-intentioned but ignorant spiritual guidance. This led them to do their best to describe what people actually experience in their journey with God. And it led John to spell out three signs that characterize the dark night of the soul.

CHAPTER FIVE

THREE SIGNS AND THREE SPIRITS

The Psychology of the Night

I can resist everything except temptation.

—*Oscar Wilde*[1] ·

A s I have said, the dark night of the soul is an ongoing transition from compulsively trying to control one's life toward a trusting freedom and openness to God and the real situations of life. It is the same in prayer, where the effort and forceful focusing of meditation are gradually eased, and the more willing receptivity of contemplation grows. In life, the process is often marked by a feeling of emptiness and lack of energy for the old ways of living. Similarly, one often experiences a growing dryness in the old ways of praying and an absence of consolation and lack of energy for meditation.

However it happens, the process is always obscure; one does not recognize what is going on. It usually feels as if there is something wrong: laziness, lassitude, depression, or some other spiritual or psychological problem. The truth is seldom even considered: that the feelings of aridity and emptiness are the birth pains of a freer life and deeper prayer. When the first glimmerings of contemplation are born, they are so dark and delicate that a person is likely to overlook them altogether. The beginning of contemplation, John says, is "secret and hidden from the very person who experiences it. . . . It is like air, which escapes if one tries to grasp it in one's hands."[2]

The Signs of the Night

In all his writings, John of the Cross's most profound concern is for those who are experiencing this obscure transition between meditation and contemplation. He says his heart is filled with "great compassion and sadness" for them when they misinterpret or fail to notice the experiences that signal this transition. John knows that the obscurity itself is evidence of God's trustworthy care, but he wants to do everything he can to make the process easier.[3]

In an attempt to help people through the confusions of the dark night in prayer, John describes three signs to help differentiate an authentic dark-night experience from other potential causes such as "sin and imperfection, weakness, lack of desire, depression *(melancholia)* or physical illness."[4]

John says the signs are for "spiritual people to notice within themselves,"[5] but in my experience it is very difficult to apply the signs to oneself. Even if all the signs are there, people are generally reluctant to claim that what they are experiencing is truly the dark night of the soul. This may be because of the continuing obscurity of the night. It may also be because claiming the night would feel arrogant. Many times I have heard people say, "The dark night is for holy people, not for me."

Perhaps, then, John's signs are more helpful in recognizing what is *not* the dark night in oneself. And as John himself seems to indicate, the signs are probably most helpful for *companions* of people going through authentic dark-night experiences. Although we may have great difficulty seeing the grace and glory of the dark night in ourselves, we can often readily identify it in another. In either case, I caution against using the signs as arbitrary criteria for "diagnosing" the dark night in oneself or another. Far better, I think, is to let what John says about the signs illuminate our appreciation of the process as a whole.

John describes the signs in slightly varying ways at different points in his writing. I have organized them here in a way that I hope will be coherent for modern readers. And although John describes them primarily in relation to the experience of prayer, I have included some experiences that may occur in other aspects of life as well.

1. Dryness and Impotence in Prayer and Life

The first sign is a diminishment of consolation in prayer and of gratification in the rest of life. In John's words, the soul "finds no consolation in things of God, nor in any created thing either."[6] Ways of meditation that used to be rewarding and rich now seem empty. Relationships and endeavors that used to be energetic and life-giving now seem to have lost their spark.

John says people experience this withering of gratification because the intellect, memory, will, and senses are generally too crude and too dulled by gross stimulations to even notice the exquisite delicacy of the deeper wisdom that God is now offering. To borrow Teresa's words, people have to lose their habitual *contentos* in order to begin to savor the *gustos* of contemplation.

Experiencing the impoverishment of their customary consolations, people usually try to renew their efforts and invest more energy, but it is to no avail. As the old pop song goes, "I can't get no satisfaction— and I try and I try . . ." They discover that no matter how hard they work at it, they just aren't able to pray or to conduct their lives in the ways they used to. John says this sign distinguishes the dryness of the dark night from that occurring with "sins and imperfections." In the latter, one usually can find some degree of satisfaction in other things and also finds it possible, after a time, to return to the old ways. But in the dark night, the old ways seem not only empty, but inaccessible as well.[7]

2. Lack of Desire for the Old Ways

At first, people usually try to recreate their old ways of prayer and living. Over time and with repeated failures, however, they recognize that such attempts come from a sense of obligation or sheer habit, not from real desire. Though they are loath to admit it, they gradually realize that they lack the motivation they once had for focused meditation and effortful striving in their lives, work, and relationships. In honesty, they come to acknowledge they really don't *want* to return to the old ways. This can be more troubling than the lack of accomplishment, because it feels like a lack of caring. "The soul," John says, "turns to God with painful concern, thinking it is not serving God but turning away." It feels like a betrayal, of God, of one's friends and enterprises, and of one's own soul. The painfulness of this realization, according to John, is an important sign that the dryness is not due to laxity or lukewarmness, in which there is no such concern. The person has by no means forgotten God, but rather remembers God with great pain and grief. Nor is the pain and grief due *solely* to depression, "melancholia, or some other humor." John says that when depression is the only cause, "there are no such desires to serve God."[8]

3. A Simple Desire to Love God

The sign that John calls the "most certain" is that
a person only desires "to remain alone in loving attentiveness to God . . . in inward peace, quietness and
rest," without any of the normal "acts and exercises"
associated with meditation and "without any particular understanding or comprehension." This desire,
John says, distinguishes the dark-night experience
from other obstacles to meditation such as depression
or some other disorder that might cause a trancelike
state or otherwise interfere with thinking.[9]

This third sign becomes especially clear in relation to the other two. Experiencing the first sign
alone, I might say, "I just can't seem to do it anymore." If someone asked me if I really *want* to do it,
I'd probably think about it a while and then sadly
admit the second sign: "No, I guess I don't really
want it anymore." Then if my questioner were to
ask me what I *really* wanted, I'd think about it some
more. I'd have to sift through all my images of what
I think prayer and life should look like. Finally I
might come to what feels like a deep-hearted desire:
"I don't know what it means or how to do it, but
what I really want is just to be with God, just to be in
love with God."

It is difficult to ask these kinds of questions of one-self in a way that encourages the careful reflection they require. One is much more likely to jump to familiar conclusions like, "I'm only being lazy" or "I just don't seem to care anymore." For this reason, it is especially helpful to have someone—a prayerful spiritual director or companion—who can ask the questions patiently and attentively. Such a companion may also help make sense of psychological reactions one might have to the experience. Some of these are so striking and common that John called them "spirits."

The Spirits of the Night

In his commentary on the first stanza of the *Dark Night* poem, John says that three spirits may visit people during the night. He does not spend a lot of time on them, but his descriptions are psychologically very precise and insightful. When I first read John's portrayal, it was clear that I knew these spirits very well. I had encountered them many times in people whom I had counseled, and I had met them frequently in myself.[10]

As troublesome as these spirits may be, John says they come from God. God uses them to further prepare the senses and faculties for the "profound wisdom and delicate exaltation" of the coming transformation. Because the intellect, memory, will, and senses are too crude and dull in the beginning of the night to appreciate the subtleties of contemplation, they need to be refined and enlivened. This, John says, is what the spirits help to do. In the long run, they exist to help. But as with so many other things in the night, this redeeming quality remains hidden; as one encounters the spirits they seem anything but helpful.

1. The Spirit of Fornication

In the popular mind, fornication means immoral sexual activity, but deeper theological considerations give the word a broader meaning. In its larger sense, fornication implies idolatry, a turning away from God and God's ways in order to seek personal gratification. This, I believe, is John's understanding when he speaks of the spirit of fornication. According to John, this spirit "buffets the soul with powerful and abominable temptations" that appeal to the imagination. Psychologically, the experience represents a desperate flailing around of the mind in the attempt to find gratification somewhere. When one repeatedly experiences dryness and emptiness in both prayer and life, it is understandable that one's imagination might run amok—as if to say, "There must be *some* way I can still get a kick out of life."[11]

A common example might be the excesses of fantasy and action that characterize what people now call a "midlife crisis." Not all such crises are part of a dark night of the soul, but some surely are, and they are characterized by a lack of gratification in work, relationships, and other endeavors. It seems only natural that when the usual means of satisfaction dry up, a person would seek others to replace them. Sometimes, however, the striving goes to such extremes of fantasy or behavior that one easily understands why John called it the spirit of fornication.

A similar thing can happen in prayer. I can recall several times when I seemed to have discovered a method of meditation that brought me significant peace and centeredness. Each time I wanted to believe that I had finally found "the way," but it would quickly dry up and become empty and boring. I would renew my efforts to no avail. Then I would look around with increasing desperation for something, anything, that might be fresh, dynamic, and exciting. In the process I always became more interested in getting a gratifying experience from prayer than in the love that had prompted the prayer in the first place. For me, there could be no more accurate definition of fornication.

2. The Spirit of Blasphemy

For John, the spirit of blasphemy is an impulse to rage against God. Whether we look at the ancient Psalms or modern headlines, it is painfully easy to see the natural outcries that accompany tragedies in life. "Why me, God?" "Where were You in my suffering?" Of course, not all tragic experiences are part of dark nights. Some lack the liberating, transforming qualities of the night. Similarly, not all rage against God is an expression of the God-given spirit of blasphemy. The God-given spirits always have a redemptive quality, in this case a refinement and sensitization of the faculties. Often, however, this is not discernible until well after the fact.

John describes the spirit of blasphemy as occurring in the context of prayer, especially in the dark night of the senses. It follows on the heels of the spirit of fornication as an understandable response to continued absence of gratification. If the prayer or meditation I've practiced in the past gave me a sense of God's presence or a secure image of God, these consolations are likely to evaporate in the night. I will try to renew my diligence and attempt other forms of meditation, but if I still find no satisfaction anywhere, anger with God is a very natural response. A spirit is hardly necessary to prompt it. I feel I have done my part, but God is not responding. Perhaps I've prayed sincerely and wholeheartedly for what I think is the experience of God, but God simply refuses to appear. Or worse, after having seemed to be present, God now goes into hiding. In the book of Jeremiah, God promises, "When you seek me with all your heart, I will let you find me" (Jer. 29:13–14). But there is another line in Jeremiah for when it seems the promise is broken: "I trusted You and You duped me!" (Jer. 20:7).

As John makes clear, it is not God who disappears, but only our concepts, images, and sensations *of* God. This relinquishment occurs to rid us of our attachment to these idols and to make possible a realization of the true God, who cannot be grasped by any thought or feeling. At the time though, it seems like abandonment, even betrayal. In the first stanza of his poem *The Spiritual Canticle*, John writes:

¿Adonde te escondiste,	Where have you hidden,
Amado, ye me dejaste	Beloved, and left me
con gemido?	moaning?
Como el ciervo huiste,	You fled like the stag
Habiéndome herido;	after wounding me;
Sali tras ti clamando,	I went out calling you,
y eras ido.	but you were gone.[12]

Similarly, consider these lines of Teresa's:

Mi alma afligida	My afflicted soul
Gime y desfallece.	Sighs and faints.
¡Ay! ¿Quien de su amado	Ah! Who, from her lover
Puede estar ausente?	Can bear to be absent?
Acabe ya, acabe.	Let it be ended, now.[13]

This poetry is hardly blasphemous, but it communicates the pain of feeling abandoned by the deepest love of one's life. John does not admit expressing anger outright. He says, "The soul is *almost* made to say [the blasphemous thoughts] aloud," and this is a "grave torment." Teresa may have been more

forthright in this. Tradition has it that after one particularly bad experience, she raised her eyes to God
and said, "If this is how you treat your friends, no
wonder you have so few of them!"[14]

3. Spiritus Vertiginis

For the third spirit, John changed from Spanish to
Latin, the language of his Bible. He took the term
spiritus vertiginis from the account in Isaiah in which
God sent a spirit of confusion, literally a "dizzy spirit,"
that made Egypt "err in everything, as a drunkard
staggers in his vomit" (Isa. 19:14).

Despite the unappealing description, the *spiritus
vertiginis* is my personal favorite. It's the one that
always does me in. It seems specifically designed for
people like me, people who refuse to relinquish the
idea that *if only I could understand things, I could make them
right*. Having lost the old willpower and its satisfactions, we desperately try to figure out where we have
gone astray. "What's happening here? Where have
I gone wrong? Maybe my problem is this . . . No,
maybe it's that . . . Perhaps I should try this . . . Or
that . . . I simply must be more diligent! Perhaps if I
tried . . ." We make countless resolutions to be more
disciplined in our lives; we read self-help books, go

to workshops, anything we can think of. It all fails, of course, and we wind up only more confused than ever. John describes it with painful accuracy: "This spirit darkens the senses and fills the person with thousands of scruples and perplexities, so confounding that they can never be satisfied with anything. . . . This is one of the most severe stimulations and horrors of this night."

Sooner or later, there is nothing left to do but give up. And that is precisely the point, the purpose of the "dizzy spirit." In each relinquishment, the person's faculties are further emptied and sensitized and, more important, reliance upon God is deepened. John says God sends this "abominable spirit" not for the soul's downfall, but to help prepare it for "union with Wisdom."

The Effects

If I understand John correctly, the three spirits work in concert with the dryness and emptiness described in the first sign of the night. The collective effect is to both invigorate and refine all of a person's faculties: intellect, memory, will, imagination, and senses. The faculties find themselves exercised and energized in their hopeless attempts to manage things. And in their failures, they become more delicate and sensitive. John says this is all in preparation for receiving the exquisite gifts of contemplation that are to come.

In essence, John recognizes that human faculties are normally neither energetic nor sensitive enough to appreciate the delicacy of contemplative consolations (Teresa's *gustos*). They have been sated with gross satisfactions and dulled by overstimulation. The dark night of the senses, through its dryness and the spirits it brings, serves to cleanse the faculties and to energize and sensitize them.

To put it in more modern psychological terms, most of us become desensitized or *habituated* to the especially delicate experiences of life. Most of us live in a world of overstimulation and sensory overload. Without realizing it, we erect defenses against our own perceptions in order to avoid being overwhelmed. To some extent, this deadens our sensitivity and dulls our perceptiveness. We find ourselves no longer appreciative of the subtle sensations, delicate fragrances, soft sounds, and exquisite feelings we enjoyed as children. Like addicts experiencing *tolerance*—the need for more and more drugs to sustain their effect—many of us find ourselves seeking increasingly powerful stimulation to keep our enjoyment and satisfaction going.[15]

It is important to remember that Teresa and John attribute these excesses to our deep, irrepressible searching for God. We are constantly trying to find ultimate satisfaction, but we unknowingly look in the wrong places. We are drawn to make idols of the good *things* of God, not knowing that it is only the *nada*, the no-thing of God's very self that can truly satisfy us. By the time life begins to break our idols, we normally find ourselves deadened and insensitive to the tender gifts we've been seeking all along. It is as if we have gorged ourselves on rich meals for so long that we cannot appreciate the delicate freshness of a sip of spring water. It is as if we have spent so long hammering in a noisy foundry that we can no longer hear the soft whisper of a breeze.

Thus John and Teresa see the "purgation" of the night as a healing process in every way. Many aspects of it may feel painful and distressing, but it is all designed for the recovery of innocence, the reestablishment of perceptiveness and sensitivity, the rebirth of profound peace and exquisite joy, and, finally, the fullness of love for God, others, and the world.

CHAPTER SIX

THE DARK NIGHT TODAY

Modern Contexts

> What whispers are these, O lands, running
>   ahead of you, passing under the seas?
> Are all nations communing? is there going to
>   be but one heart to the globe?
>
> —*Walt Whitman*[1]

Teresa and John demonstrate an understanding of human psychology that seems uncanny for their era. They knew the workings of the human unconscious four centuries before Sigmund Freud. With amazing accuracy they described psychological phenomena that would later be called defense mechanisms, behavioral conditioning, addictive and affective disorders, and psychosis. And in my opinion, they had clearer insights into the dynamics of consciousness and attention than most modern neuroscientists do.

I think there are several reasons Teresa and John were such excellent psychologists. First, like other contemplatives, they learned their psychology firsthand, through acute, extended, and direct attentiveness to their own interior lives. They reflected upon this experience, seeking to comprehend and integrate its meaning and to articulate it in ways that would make sense to others. In addition, they were deeply immersed in community. As spiritual directors they attended to the inner lives of numerous individuals, and as community leaders they were intensely involved in the teamwork, power struggles, and other dimensions of group dynamics. Just as important, Teresa and John had exquisite gifts for communicating their insights through poetry, story, metaphor, and concept.

For me it is an irresistibly delicious idea to reflect on Teresa's and John's insights in the light of modern psychology and to ponder how they might react to the scientific advances of the last four centuries. The possibilities for such reflections are endless, but I will limit my discussion here to five contemporary contexts: depression, addiction, personality and gender, spiritual companionship, and social systems.

The Dark Night and Depression

It is by no means a new idea that the dark night of the soul can be confused with depression. In some ways, this was even more of a concern for Teresa and John than it is today. In sixteenth-century Spain, people were far more likely to spiritualize mental illness, to attribute it to angelic or demonic forces. Teresa and John were vitally concerned that people who suffered from *melancholia* or "some other bad humor" be accurately diagnosed and receive the treatment they needed. This was one of John's primary motivations in developing his three signs of the night, and both he and Teresa had many other insights about distinguishing debilitating depression from more liberating spiritual experiences.[2]

In my earlier book *Care of Mind, Care of Spirit*, I attempted to clarify the distinction between the dark night and depression in modern psychological terms. I said, for example, that a person's sense of humor, general effectiveness, and compassion for others are not usually impaired in the dark night as they are in depression. There is also often a sense that down deep, people really wouldn't trade their experience of the dark night for more pleasure—it's as if at some level they sense the rightness of it. And I mentioned that in accompanying people through dark-night experiences, I never felt the negativity and resentment I often felt when working with depressed people.[3]

But it is not quite so simple. Perhaps the distinctions I have made, supplementing those that Teresa and John give, might help distinguish depression from the dark night of the soul when there is no overlap. But my experience is that people often experience depression and the dark night at the same time. To say the least, the dark night can be depressing. Even if most of the experience feels liberating, it still involves loss, and loss involves grief, and grief may at least temporarily become depression. Conversely, a primary clinical depression can become part of a dark-night experience, just as any other illness can.

John clearly acknowledges this overlap. In discussing the second sign of the night, he says the pain and grief "may sometimes be increased by melancholy or some other humor . . . [and] frequently is."[4]

Since the dark night and depression so often coexist, trying to distinguish one from the other is not as helpful as it might first appear. With today's understanding of the causes and treatment of depression, it makes more sense simply to identify depression where it exists and to treat it appropriately, regardless of whether it is associated with a dark-night experience.

I want to restate this, because it can prevent unnecessary suffering and in some cases even be lifesaving. If someone is experiencing symptoms of significant depression, it is important that those symptoms be recognized and acknowledged, and that the person receive at least a psychiatric consultation concerning treatment. It's wonderful if the same person happens to be experiencing something of the dark night of the soul as well, but the presence of the dark night should not cause any hesitation about treating depression. Because of recently developed medications, depression is now recognized as a very treatable disorder, and it is a crime to let it go unattended.

The signs of clinical depression are becoming well known these days and are generally recognizable in oneself or others if time is taken to consider them. They include such symptoms as difficulty concentrating and making decisions, persistent sadness, hopelessness, anxiety, pessimism, guilt or a feeling of worthlessness, fatigue and lack of energy, insomnia, early morning awakening or oversleeping, decreased appetite and weight loss or overeating and weight gain, thoughts of death or suicide, and various persistent physical symptoms that do not respond to treatment.[5]

There is a persisting notion in some circles that the medications used to treat depression and other psychiatric illnesses can somehow interfere with deeper spiritual processes such as the dark night. Nothing could be further from the truth. To my mind, there is never an authentic spiritual reason to let any illness go untreated. John himself says that even if the cleansing grief of the night is compounded by melancholia it "does not fail . . . since the desire remains centered upon God." The sensory part of the soul, he says, may be "weak and enfeebled, but the spirit is ready and strong."[6]

I am not certain why people still think that medications can interfere with God's work in human souls. Perhaps it is because medications are frequently abused and sometimes substituted for the spiritual consolations people seek. Or perhaps it is the memory of older psychiatric medications that accomplished little but sedation. More likely, it is probably due to the persisting ancient dualism between matter and spirit—that things of the flesh like chemicals can have nothing but a negative effect upon the "higher" things of the spirit. In order to believe this, though, one's theology would have to hold that God's grace is so weak and ineffective that a chemical compound can block it. Teresa and John left that kind of thinking behind four centuries ago, and it is high time for modern people to catch up with them.

There are some signs that we are beginning to catch up. One example is a statement made by author Judith Hooper. After interviewing a collection of psychiatrists and Buddhist practitioners about depression, Hooper concluded, "Before enlightenment, take Prozac and talk to your shrink. After enlightenment, take Prozac and talk to your shrink."[7]

The Dark Night and Addiction

In discussing attachment, Teresa and John used combinations of words like *afición* ("fondness"), *afección* ("affection"), and *asimiento* ("grasping"). The terms communicate a wide range of attraction from simple enjoyment to the choiceless compulsions that today we would call addiction. I have discussed the way in which attachments bind the energy of the human spirit and create idols to which we become enslaved. It is precisely from such enslavement that the dark night works to free us.

Modern psychology and neurology have shed considerable light on how attachments and addictions form in the nervous system. We now know many of the specific kinds of molecular changes that take place in nerve cells in the presence of addictive chemicals and behaviors, as well as the mechanisms of withdrawal symptoms. With all its technological advances, however, neuroscience has yet to produce a cure for addiction.[8]

Nor has medical science been able to replace the essential spiritual nature of recovery from addiction. To date, the most effective addiction treatments rely upon the twelve-step model originally developed in the 1930s as Alcoholics Anonymous. The first three of these steps are strikingly reminiscent of the language of the dark night. They so clearly portray the transition from personal effort to spiritual receptivity that they might well have been written by Teresa or John:

1. We admitted we were powerless over alcohol—
    that our lives had become unmanageable.

2. We came to believe that a Power greater
    than ourselves could restore us to sanity.

3. We made a decision to turn our will and
    our lives over to the care of God as we
    understood Him.

No one understands the dark night of the soul
better than people recovering from life-threatening
addictions. Some AA members call themselves
"grateful alcoholics" because their addiction finally
brought them to their knees. It was only because of
the addiction that they discovered the true depths
and longings of their souls.

Such spiritual awakenings can sometimes lead to
another kind of dark night, what I've called a "dark
night of recovery." To understand it, we need to
realize that twelve-step programs "work" best when
people have come to know without doubt that recovery is a life-or-death matter, that dependence upon
the Higher Power is the only way to life. This is a
special kind of beginning for a spiritual journey.
There are no delicate mysterious inner longings here,

only the simple, desperate need to stay alive. As long as this sense of absolute necessity continues, a person can work the steps of the program with complete dedication to recovery. Whatever images of God the person may have earlier held, God now is the Higher Power, the source of the grace one needs for recovery, the only hope for survival.

Many people continue in recovery this way for years—perhaps for their whole lives. Others, however, experience something different at a certain point along the way. After having worked the program for a while, a person may begin to notice that what began as a desperate *need* for God is changing into a loving *desire* for God. It is as if God were saying, "Of course I want to be your saving Higher Power. But I also want to be so much more to you. I want to be your deepest love." And somehow, something in the person's heart has become free enough to say yes to this barely heard invitation. In the dark night's characteristic obscurity, compulsion is again becoming freedom, necessity changing into choice.

Before, one needed God as the agent of recovery, the divine dispenser of grace. Now this need is developing into a love for God as God's self. This is a beautiful happening, but it brings with it a new relinquishment that can feel deeply threatening. Along with the sweetness of emerging love comes a certain shakiness about recovery. Recovery is no longer the single most important thing in life. Something else has taken its place, and the fear of relapse grows.

Later, one may come to realize that recovery, as the most important thing in life, had become an idol. God was a means to an end—recovery. Then in darkness, after the heart said yes and love grew, the idol of recovery teetered and fell. The powers had shifted. Recovery is now no longer the end, but only a means in the service of love.

All the signs of the night are there in this transition. What had worked before no longer does, and one's previous energetic dedication is waning. More disturbing still, the deep care, the desperate need for recovery seems undermined. And if given the unusual insight and courage to admit it, one would have to say the deepest desire is no longer for recovery, but for God alone.

I have walked with several people through this particularly blessed and troublesome night. All were terrified of relapse, and some temporarily did relapse. But all made it through to deeper freedom: freedom not only from their enslavement to addiction, but also freedom from their servitude to recovery. Now their gratitude is not only for the grace of recovery, but even more for the simple freedom to love God and their neighbors more completely.[9]

Personality and Gender and the Dark Night

Like snowflakes, no two human beings are exactly alike. Yet just as scientists categorize snowflakes according to their shape (plates, dendrites, columns, etc.), popular psychology classifies people according to a wide variety of characteristics. Racial and ethnic categorization, widespread in years past, is now often considered unfair and potentially dangerous. More recently it has become popular to categorize people psychologically according to characteristics of gender, personality, and temperament. Women, for example, are thought to be generally more in touch with their feelings than are men. People in the "4" category of the Enneagram system tend to be dramatic and have a need to feel special. An introvert on the Meyers-Briggs scale tends to be uncomfortable in large groups. Although a few such characterizations (such as introversion and extraversion) have statistical validity, most do not. Still, many people find the distinctions useful in understanding themselves and their relationships with others.

As the insightful psychologists that they were, Teresa and John would probably not be surprised at modern society's interest in how human personalities are so alike and yet so different. I imagine they would be fascinated with all the measurements we've invented and with the plethora of labels we put on ourselves. I can almost see Teresa savoring the new vocabulary.

I think, however, that Teresa and John would disapprove of attempts to extend such categorizations to the spiritual life and would be especially put off by prescription of spiritual practices on the basis of personality characteristics. "That's God's business," they would say. I'm putting words in their mouths here, but I believe this response is consistent with what they have written. Again and again they emphasize the uniqueness of each person's nature and the singular way in which God acts in each person's life. For them, it is not simply human diversity that accounts for different experiences; it is the way God's "esteeming love" moves with total respect for the precious identity of each person. I think this is the reason that Teresa and John make few suggestions and virtually no specific prescriptions as to ways of prayer and meditation. Do what brings you most to love, they say, and let God do the rest.

Still, it seems clear that Teresa and John could readily identify with some of the modern literature on human differences, especially in the area of gender. Although John does not describe his own personal experience in much detail, it seems that he views the spiritual life as being a generally humbling process. The ego seems to begin in a state of some arrogance, feeling it can chart its own course and master its destiny. Life and prayer teach it otherwise and bring it—often kicking and screaming—to its knees in surrender. Only in the dawn after the night, in the realization of union, is the soul able to claim its true goodness, beauty, and value. This process is certainly in keeping with the most popular modern views of men's spiritual experience, which portray a journey from delusional arrogance through humiliation to self-acceptance.

Teresa tells us more about her life experience, and much of it seems to be what today might be called a "woman's story" of spiritual liberation. Rather than starting in arrogance, Teresa seems to have begun her intentional spiritual life doubting herself and putting her trust in others. Her journey then seems to be more one of empowerment, of claiming her own judgments and finding her confidence and voice. I may be stretching for conclusions here, yet I can't deny that Teresa's and John's stories do convey some resonance with modern gender understandings.

As with personality labeling, there is always a temptation to jump from an appreciation of gender differences to a diagnostic or prescriptive frame of mind. I think Teresa and John would balk at any statement that implies, "Because you're a woman [or man], your spiritual life and experience will be like this." Again they would affirm that the particular path a person's soul life follows is determined by God's unique, loving, and *always unpredictable* attentiveness.

According to Teresa and John, the deepest constants of the spiritual life are the same for everyone regardless of personality or gender. It's always a process of liberation from attachment, of growing freedom for love of God and person, of self-knowledge and the realization of one's true identity in God. And a large part of it always takes place in obscurity. Beyond those common foundations, however, our individual stories are colored and textured by who we are as individuals and by God's unique ways of loving us—ways that can never be prescribed, only discovered.

Spiritual Companionship and the Dark Night

Nowhere did Teresa and John express their concern for human uniqueness as strongly as in their ministries of spiritual companionship. They offered spiritual direction to countless people, not only to other vowed members of religious orders, but also to many laypeople. Both were very sensitive to the potential help—and harm—that such relationships could provide. Teresa, as we have seen, had more than her share of troublesome experiences with her own directors. Although we know little of John's experience in receiving direction, his writings make clear that he companioned many people who had previously been hurt by bad direction. Of all the contributions Teresa and John have made to our appreciation of the spiritual life, their insights into spiritual companionship are second only to their wisdom about personal prayer.

As a general recommendation, both Teresa and John advocate finding a spiritual director who is both "learned" from an academic and scriptural standpoint and "experienced" in his or her own prayer life. They agree that it may be difficult to find both of these qualities in one person and recommend consulting with more than one director as needed. Most important, the choice of a director should be made prayerfully and carefully, since misdirection happens frequently and can be very harmful. "Be careful," says Teresa, "not to choose someone who will teach you to become a toad, satisfied only with catching little lizards."[10]

From their writings, it is clear that Teresa and John felt the most prevalent error of spiritual directors was trying to do too much, meddling with the precious work of God in a soul. When this happens, John says, it is like a beautiful and exquisite painting's being roughened and discolored by a "crude hand" that knows nothing of art.[11]

This is critical wisdom for contemporary times. Given the popularity of modern psychological theory, the tendency of spiritual directors to meddle with

God's work is worse today than it ever was. Our knowledge of psychology gives us such a huge kit of tools for analyzing and attempting to control our spiritual lives that it can be irresistibly tempting to turn spiritual direction into a masquerade of psychotherapy. Thus it is crucial that spiritual directors always remember that they are attending to God's work in souls, not their own. John has no mercy for spiritual directors who assume they know or can figure out what is right for their companions. He calls them "pests" and "blind guides" and likens them to "blacksmiths who know only how to hammer and pound with the faculties."[12]

Understandably, John was especially troubled about spiritual directors interfering with people's experience of the dark night of the soul. With the ignorant collusion of their spiritual directors, people might turn away from the obscure invitations of God in the night, a possibility that he said brought "great pity and compassion to my heart." For this reason, John included a substantial digression in his commentary on *The Living Flame of Love*, in which he described some of the most common and harmful mistakes made by directors. These observations are at least as applicable now as they were in John's time.[13]

First, he underscores that it is God, not the person and certainly not the director, who is the primary mover and initiator of the soul's transformation. God "guides the blind soul, taking it by the hand to the place it does not know." Both the person and the director are likely to misinterpret experiences along this journey. The drying up of meditation and other practices, accompanied by diminished motivation, often feels like resistance, lassitude, and insufficient discipline. The person is likely to want to renew his or her willpower and dedication to get things back to the way they were. Unless directors are especially humble and prayerful, they are apt to collude in such attempts at problem solving. Instead, they should gently help those they counsel to reflect on what their real desire seems to be, what their deepest inclinations are. Here, as discussed in the last chapter, the spiritual companion's most helpful role may be to ask the questions that elucidate John's second and third signs of the night: "Do you really want to go back to the way things were?" and "What, then, do you most deeply desire?"

Encouraging this kind of reflection requires that spiritual directors restrain their knee-jerk tendencies to diagnose and fix problems. At times this may be quite difficult. There are prolonged periods in spiritual direction, for example, when it seems a person is becoming stagnated, making no progress. But spiritual "progress" has some unique qualities. Especially in the dark night, it is hidden. It happens in secret places in the soul where, as John says, "neither the intellect nor the devil" can touch it. Moreover, it often feels like regression. Not only do people discover a diminishment in intentional practice, but those who have been making psychological progress in claiming and asserting their own authority may find themselves becoming more passive and accepting in relation to others. John maintains that in the transitions of the night, it is right and proper for the soul to endure what seems like stagnation or lack of intention. "Do not say, 'Oh, the soul is making no progress because it isn't doing anything,'" John advises, "for I will prove to you that the soul is doing a great deal by doing nothing." What looks like stagnation or regression, then, may well be the surface appearance of a secret willingness, a yes for God to do what God will in one's heart.

The same applies when people lose the concepts and images about God that have served them so well in the past. It is not at all uncommon in experiences of the night for individuals to doubt that they even believe in God anymore because all the signs and hallmarks of what they considered to be their faith are disappearing. Yet to a perceptive companion, the love for God is still there, and stronger than ever in the concern and yearning felt by the individuals. John counsels that this loss of belief is also a good sign. Because "God transcends the intellect," the mind must be emptied "of everything it comprehends."

In general, John advises spiritual directors to recognize that the souls in their care need to be able to respond to God's deep invitations, often without understanding them. They need to let those souls be free in all ways: free to make life decisions that may not make sense to the director, and free to seek direction elsewhere. When a person wants to leave a direction relationship, the director should support the decision and not be possessive or jealous.

All of this, as I have said, can be very difficult for spiritual companions, especially for spiritual directors who try to be "professionals" in the modern sense of the word. They want to provide a good, helpful service and to see themselves as doing a good job. Surely this is a responsible and caring attitude in most situations, but neither Teresa nor John would accept it as an excuse for overzealous meddling in a soul's spiritual journey. "Each soul is God's own," they would say. "Not one of them belongs to you."

The Dark Night and Social Systems

Teresa and John were immersed in social and political conflicts and reforms as their life work, but there is little in their writings to indicate much reflection about social or political systems beyond the dynamics of living in a religious community. John barely touches on the subject, and Teresa's descriptions of political encounters are almost always unpleasant. Recounting the lawsuits and intrigues necessary for the foundation of her little convents she complains, "Oh Jesus, what a trial it is to deal with so many opinions!"[14]

Instead of looking into social and political dynamics specifically, Teresa and John keep returning to the experience of the individual soul in relationship to God. I have found this to be true of other contemplative writers as well. It is not that they are unconcerned with social liberation and justice, but that they are convinced such transformation will happen only through the changing of individual hearts. The Dalai Lama put it starkly in 1991: "Although attempting to bring about world peace through the internal transformation of individuals is difficult, it is the only way."[15]

For Teresa and John, social and political systems seemed to function primarily as contexts, environments within which individual people live and move. Those environments can be helpful or harmful to people's well-being, supportive or antagonistic toward the nurturance of love. Teresa began her reform of the Carmelites precisely to create communities that would be more conducive to their members' inner growth in love for God and one another.

In this regard, I think Teresa and John would have been entranced by twentieth-century social systems theories, which propose that any grouping of people is more than the sum of its parts; it is a system with its own life, an entity in many ways like a person. Each family, community, church, business, even nation or culture has characteristics and experiences that constitute a life of its own. Like the individuals who make them up, groups can be seen as growing and learning, yearning and dreaming, decaying and dying.[16]

An obvious question in this context is whether social systems might be said to have (or be) souls, and if so, whether they might experience something equivalent to a corporate dark night of the soul. If a group derives its being, energy, and characteristics from the mutual interactions of its constituents, then it can be said to have at least some soul qualities. More important to my mind are the actual experiences that occur in social systems. Some of these are undeniably similar to dark-night experiences.

Certainly marriages and families encounter times when ways of relating that worked well in the past seem to dry up. Old ways of satisfaction become empty. As with individuals experiencing dark nights, the first assumption is usually that there's something wrong, and the parties try to discover the problem and correct it. They read books on how to put the zest back in their relationship, how to rediscover romance, how to cope with midlife, and so on. And, as in the dark night, such attempts frequently fail.

Also like the night, these experiences are often obscure. The people involved feel confused, mystified, unable to get a grasp of what is actually going on, much less how to respond to it. This happens frequently in corporate and religious organizations as well. Something shifts somewhere, things are not as they used to be, people lose touch with goals and mission, everything seems to have lost its moorings. More times than I can count, the *spiritus vertiginis* has visited organizations of which I've been a member. The other spirits seem to visit social systems too. Fornication manifests in extreme and bizarre attempts to force *some* kind of success or gratification *somewhere*. Blasphemy brings blaming, rage, vengefulness, and the feeling of wanting to cash it all in. And it always feels like something is wrong.

These phenomena can also be seen in national and cultural systems. Few would doubt that Western society has been undergoing the painful demise of old values and traditions, and the new substitutes generally don't seem promising. This is of course nothing new; humanity has been through such cycles many times before. On each occasion though, the question seems to deepen: Can we fix it this time? Is there really any way out?

All of these considerations contribute to a very tempting possibility: maybe some—perhaps many—of the troubles we experience collectively are really manifestations of a communal dark night of the soul. If so, then some of the turmoil we experience in marriages, families, organizations, or cultures might not be due to something gone terribly wrong. It might be a sign of something going exquisitely *right,* of divine action carrying us darkly through spaces where we would not and could not go on our own, toward a place of greater freedom and love.

The hope is so enticing and sometimes the signs seem so undeniable that I cannot help but believe it is true. But of course we don't know for sure. Especially if the dark night *is* at work, we can never really know. We have to be careful, I think, about overanthropomorphizing social groups. And if we really want to get a glimpse of dark-night possibilities, we need to look for what John offers as signs of the night.

The first sign—the drying up of gratifications and the powerlessness to do anything about it—seems present in a wide variety of social situations in which I've found myself. It seems true not just for individuals, but for the group as a whole. Often the second sign also seems true: there is a lack of deep-down motivation to return to the old ways. They just don't hold the promise they once did.

It is the third and, as John says, "the surest" sign that catches me up. Is there a deep heartfelt desire within the community or group to "remain alone in loving awareness of God . . . in interior peace and stillness, without the acts and exercises"? Here I stumble. What might this heartfelt desire look like in a marriage, in a corporation, in a nation? I find I cannot really comprehend it.

Surely most social systems do not seem to be seeking a particular deity. But John affirms that the "loving awareness" does not have to be associated with any specific image of God. Finally, in fact, it cannot be any image at all, for God is *nada,* no-thing. So it is impossible to judge the deeper desires of a system, if indeed they exist, on the basis of religious ideology. It is neither the *name* (God, Allah, or Krishna) nor the *man* (Jesus or Buddha) that is the final object of this loving desire. It is something far deeper and far greater than any identification whatsoever. And it makes me wonder: maybe, when people long for sheer love and bare compassion, when they yearn for simplicity of being and naturalness of peace, when they die inside from the simple desire for liberty and justice, maybe that might become manifest in their relationships, in the groups they form, and maybe— just maybe—that might be the third and surest sign.

There is no way to be certain, but the possibility leaves me with a glimpse of incredible hope in situations that seem the most hopeless. As we continue our relentless struggles to understand what's going on and to fix things to the best of our ability, perhaps a dark night of the soul is always going on as well. Maybe, sometimes, in the midst of things going terribly wrong, something is going just right. But that's the devil of it; there is no way to know for sure. All we can do is hope for the dawn.

CHAPTER SEVEN

DAYBREAK

The Coming of the Dawn

The glory of God is a human being fully alive.

—*Ireneaus*[1]

Just as experiences of the night are dark because of
their obscurity, experiences of the dawn are times
of light, of seeing things more clearly. John is quick
to say that the clarity of the dawn is not complete.
The light, although divine, is not like the fierce sun of
midday. It is, instead, a muted light of "early morning" or "rising dawn." It continues to partake of
some of the night's mystery. Comprehension remains
absent, of course, but there is an appreciation that
John likens to opening one's eyes to unexpected light.

The dawn is an awakening to a deepening realization of who we really are in and with God and the world, and of what has been going on within us in the night. Always, and most important, the dawn is an awakening in love.[2]

Contemplatives of all traditions agree on one certain thing—the spiritual life is all about love. Thus the dark night of the soul exists for the sole purpose of furthering love, a love that is partially realized in each experience of the dawn. In the last verse of his final poem, John writes of this awakening:

How gently and lovingly
you wake in my heart,
where in secret you dwell alone;
and in your sweet breathing,
filled with good and glory,
how tenderly you swell my heart with love.[3]

This love, divine in its nature and glimpsed only through the gift of divine light, is the greatest of all mysteries. It is the source, means, and end of all life, yet no one can explain or define it. The Buddhist understanding of compassion and the Christian notion of *agape* (divine love) perhaps come as close as human conception can. But love's true nature remains forever beyond the grasp of all our faculties. It is far greater than any feeling or emotion and completely surpasses any act of human kindness. It is the one sheer gift of contemplation, completely unattainable by autonomous human effort. The realization of this love always remains mysterious. We may fall into it, wake up within it, discover that it pervades us, but no matter how we might try, we can never reduce it to an object for study or definition. It is indeed the breath of the Divine, and John says he does not even wish to speak of it lest he "make it appear less than it is."[4]

Although the love itself remains indescribable, the morning light does reveal some things that have been happening within us—things that no doubt have been readying and opening us to more fully participate in this immense love. These are somewhat more comprehensible than the love itself, so I will try to say a few things about just three of them.

One of the developments that the morning light reveals is growing freedom, experienced as the energy of desire is liberated from the attachments that have kept it restrained. A second change is the classical transition from meditation to contemplation in prayer and the equivalent movement in the rest of life: a metamorphosis of the soul from autonomous self-determination to self-giving willingness to be led. A third change is the awakening itself: the dawning realization of our essential union with God and all creation.

It seems to me that each of these three changes is necessary to prepare us for deepening participation in love. Freedom from attachment enables love to be noncompelled. For most of us, the notion of love without attachment is inconceivable. Where would our motivation for loving feelings and actions come from, if not from attachment? Some Buddhists say that true compassion is the essence of creation. Thus, if allowed to remain free from our own ego agendas, it will arise directly and spontaneously within every situation. John says our participation in love comes directly from God's own love, and that, when freed from our personal attachments, our motivations become indistinguishable from God's own.

This immediately points out the necessity of the second change, from meditative willfulness to contemplative willingness. If we were left in the realm of self-determination, our freedom would remain directionless. It might be freedom *from* attachment, but it would not be freedom *for* anything. It would be doomed to wander from one self-generated intention to the next. It is only by moving from self-determination to divinely inspired participation that freedom finds its direction toward the fulfillment of love.

And it is the realization of our essential union with God and creation that enables and empowers the practical living of love in the real situations of life. There is no missionary zeal here, no knee-jerk attempts to be helpful, no programmed acts of religious nicety, no knowledge of what to do for one's neighbor. Here actions and feelings flow from a bottomless source within us, and our intellect can do nothing but stand by and marvel. Moments such as these are what Teresa calls participation in God. In John's understanding, they are the result of the intellect's becoming faith, the memory's becoming hope, and the will's becoming love.

I am convinced that we experience such moments more frequently than we think. We often have trouble recognizing them, in part because they are so short-lived and in part because they don't fit our normal understandings of life. We literally can make nothing of them, so they often go unnoticed. And of course we can't make them happen. Part of the spiritual life process, I think, is coming to recognize such moments when they are given, and to savor and claim them. They will probably always remain intermittent and transient. Perhaps we can take comfort in knowing that the longest they ever lasted for a great saint such as Teresa was about half an hour. But however short-lived they may be, these repeated dawning realizations have a profound effect upon us. They let us know what we are for: the reason for our being. And by so doing, they affirm and empower that deep yes within us, the desire that is our hope, our prayer, and our meaning.

Morning Comes Every Day

I have repeatedly suggested that, contrary to popular assumptions, the dark night is not a single event in one's life that one undergoes and then somehow moves beyond. Instead, I have characterized the night as *the* ongoing spiritual process of our lives. We have periodic conscious experiences of it, but it continues at all times, hidden within us. We are aware of only the experiences that come to our consciousness. Thus what someone else might call "going through the dark night" I would call "having an experience of the dark night." At first this may sound like a minor semantic distinction, but I think the difference is important. Life is not a matter of reaching a stagnant end point, but is rather an ongoing process in which one, hopefully and with grace, grows ever more deeply in love.

If indeed we have intermittent conscious experiences of the always ongoing dark night, then experiences of the dawn must happen periodically and repeatedly as well. We have already seen how Teresa affirms this in saying that no one becomes so advanced that they don't often have to return to the beginning. She further validates repeated experiences of the dawn in describing how brief her own experiences of union are, and in saying that God presents God's self as a bridegroom for the soul "very commonly" and in varying degrees of depth.[5]

John also describes an intermittent quality of realization in speaking of the dark night of the senses. God brings souls, he says, "at times and for short periods, into this night of contemplation and purgation . . . causing the night to come upon them, and then dawn, frequently."[6]

In practical terms, this means that just as we often experience the obscurity and confusion of the dark night, we are also often given experiences of the dawn. To some extent, the dawn experiences may constitute what Teresa calls the *gustos* of contemplation, the indescribable delight of God's own joy overflowing into our senses. But it is also much more, and Teresa and John use many metaphors to try to describe it. John speaks of the soul's being like a log set afire, slowly warming, steaming, lighting, blazing, and finally being transformed into God's own fire of love. He also likens the soul to a window, being so cleansed in the process of the night that finally it coalesces indistinguishably with the light of God that shines through it. Perhaps Teresa's most famous metaphor is that of the silkworm, slowly transformed in the darkness of its cocoon, emerging as a butterfly, fluttering about, and finally finding its rightful place in divine realization.[7]

One image of the dawn that I especially like, and one they both use, is the sparrow on the high roof from Psalm 102: "I watch, and am as a sparrow alone on the housetop" (v. 7). Teresa says of her own experience, "It seems to me that the soul is not in itself at all, but high on its rooftop, raised above all created things, even above its own highest part." And according to John, "At the coming of dawn . . . the mind, in sweet tranquillity, is elevated above its comprehension to a divine light." He then goes on to enumerate five somewhat quaint ways in which the soul at dawn is like the sparrow on the rooftop. First, he says, as the sparrow likes high places, so the soul rises to "the highest contemplation." Second, as the sparrow turns its face toward the wind, the soul turns toward the "Spirit of Love, which is God." Third, the soul is solitary in contemplation, as the sparrow is alone on the housetop. Fourth, as the sparrow sings sweetly, so does the soul sing praises of the "sweetest love." And finally John says the sparrow is "of no particular color," and neither is the soul in this state, for it has gone beyond all sensate things.[8]

In the end, of course, the best images and metaphors can only point in the general direction of the actual experience of dawn. Further, I am certain that we have many different experiences of the night and of the morning. No two people's experiences will ever be identical, and each of our own experiences will be different from one time to the next. Some are likely to be outstanding, dramatic, and memorable, while others—perhaps most—will be so delicate and transient that they are nearly unrecognized. Yet all share some elements of the three qualities I have described: freedom, realization, and the easing of willfulness that characterizes contemplation. And all such moments, we can hope, will somehow find their way into deepening love in the actions of our lives.

Hope in the Morning

I find it almost unbearably tempting to try to identify how the ongoing process of the night increases our love. Looking at communities, organizations, nations, and the world at large I have to say it is very difficult to discover. If a growing love is there at all, I think, it is hidden beyond my perception. This makes me wonder if the dark night really applies only to individual souls. Then I reflect back over my own life, in which it seems I can identify many experiences of both night and morning, and I ask, "Am I really more loving now than I used to be?" Sometimes I think I am; other times I'm not at all so sure. And then, finally, I remember how vast and incomprehensible real love is, and how terribly limited is my capacity to judge it for myself, let alone for anyone else. My ideas of love have to do with emotional feelings and acts of kindness, and I know these bear as much similarity to divine love as Teresa's silkworm does to the butterfly. And I am reminded of how attached I am to the idea of progress; I am looking for objective evidence that I am making headway in this spiritual journey. Yet the truth of the journey admits of no such evidence, and it completely transcends my petty notions of progress.

So in the end I am left only with hope. I hope the nights really are transformative. I hope every dawn brings deeper love, for each of us individually and for the world as a whole. I hope that John of the Cross was right when he said the intellect is transformed into faith, and the will into love, and the memory into . . . hope.

I sense that there is something very special about the transformed qualities of faith, love, and hope. This is very hard to describe, and my attempts always feel shabby, but I must try. In their truly contemplative and transformed state, faith, hope, and love are tied to no particular ends; they have no object. Contemplative faith is not faith that God exists, that life is essentially good, or that this or that is true. All such things are *beliefs*, not faith. Faith is, instead, a way of being, completely open, empty, as John would say, of all specifics. Contemplative faith is more like a continual fire of goodness, warming and illuminating every breath. Contemplative love is completely beyond comprehension. It is not love of some things to the exclusion of others, for that would be attachment. True love is like some infinite way of being that we become part of: a flowing energy of willingness, an eternal yes resounding with every heartbeat. And contemplative hope, the transformed hope, is also completely open and free. It is not hope *for* peace or justice or healing; that also would be attachment. It is *just* hope, naked hope, a bare energy of open expectancy.

I think I have experienced this kind of transformed hope from time to time in people who have suffered more than anyone deserves. And when I saw it in them, I was blinded. An old priest, abandoned by his community, sick and dying and terribly depressed, lifted his eyes and whispered, "Oh, Jesus, I do love you so." He smiled at me, his face was filled with hope, and his smile filled me with hope. And in the summer of 1994 I joined a small pilgrimage to Bosnia. I had the opportunity to speak with poor people who had lost everything: homes, possessions, entire families. As they told us their stories through tears of grief, I sensed deep hope in them. Through interpreters I asked if it were true.

"Yes, hope," they smiled.

I asked if it was hope for peace.

"No, things have gone too far for that."

I asked if they hoped the United Nations or the United States would intervene in some positive way.

"No, it's too late for that."

I asked them, "Then, what is it you are hoping for?"

They were silent. They could not think of a thing to hope for, yet there it was—undeniable hope shining in them.

I asked one last question. "How can you hope, when there's nothing to hope for?"

The answer was, "Bog," the Serbo-Croatian word for God.

Thus I have had some glimpses into the nature of this transformed hope. I believe I have experienced moments of it myself, but I can neither fathom nor comprehend it. Like contemplative faith and love, it evades my understanding. The one thing I can say positively about these transformed qualities is that to discover them, in oneself or in another, brings the deepest reassurance I have ever experienced.

So What?

I f there were such a thing as a divine suggestion box, I'd suggest that God make things easier. Or if not easier, at least clearer. I would love to close this book with something more substantial than empty faith, unattached love, and hopeless hope. I would love to be able to make practical suggestions about how to identify and claim the transformative qualities of the dark night in your own life. I yearn to offer something that would really make the hard times easier and bring a definite sense of meaning to the unavoidable sufferings of life. It would be so wonderful to be able to prescribe effective methods or understandings that could help us all get a grip on our destinies. But the nature of the dark night does not permit that. It comes as gift and in obscurity, as and when it will, taking us where we would not and could not go on our own. And though in truth we say yes to it, we have little or no control over it. The reason for the obscurity, John says, is to keep us safe, so we don't stumble because we think we know where we're going. I do want to trust that.

All we have in our own hands is our desire, which is at once our prayer, our yes, and our hope. For me, in the good times, hope is synonymous with trust. I move into the next moment with confidence and an expectation of goodness. In the hard times, hope takes on an increasing feeling of risk. I hope for the best, but the next moment feels uncertain, even scary. And in the worst of times, the hope and desire may be reduced to a bare ember, so faint as to be almost undetectable. But it is always there, and sooner or later we are drawn to it. I believe that with repeated experiences of touching that desire, we do learn to recognize it, claim it, and know it as who we really are. Maybe, in a way, that is a kind of progress.

The Vulnerability of God

Since I cannot end with methods of making things better, I want to share one final observation that the contemplatives have to offer us. In a way, it brings us back to where I began this book, with Rabbi Kushner's statement that our sympathetic response to life's unfairness may be the surest proof of God's reality.

It is usual for people to think of God as the Supreme Being, the Lord and Master of all Creation, the omnipotent Higher Power who is in charge of everything. Such a God is separate from us, transcendent, above and beyond us, and capable of giving us good things and bad things. We naturally pray for the good things we want and for relief from the bad things we don't want. And usually it doesn't work. We don't get all we want, and we get too much of what we don't want. Logically then, that transcendent, omnipotent, and separate God seems arbitrary at best, unloving at worst.

But the contemplatives, as we have seen with Teresa and John, emphasize God's immanence as well as transcendence. God is our center, they say, closer to us than we are to ourselves. We are immersed in God, and God is immersed in us. So if the transcendent God "out there" is arbitrary or unloving to us, that same God is being arbitrary or unloving to the God "in here." An alternative vision, one that I find repeatedly in contemplative literature, is that instead of God's being unloving or arbitrary, God may not be so omnipotent. Or at least the power of God may not extend to making God invulnerable. Most contemplatives see God as being wounded when and as we are wounded, sharing our sufferings as well as our joys. When bad things happen to us, they also happen to God. This is certainly in keeping with Teresa's sense of the Holy One's being surrendered to us in love and *needing* us to love, to be loved by, and to manifest God's love in the world.

The idea of God's having any needs at all, let alone needing us, may sound like an alien, even heretical idea, yet it is a realization that many contemplatives come to. Theologically, if God is indeed all-loving—if God *is* Love—then that love must necessarily temper God's omnipotence. Love always transforms power, making it something softer, deeper, and richer. Conversely, it may be only in our vulnerability, in our actually *being* wounded, that love gains its full power. Thus true omnipotence may not be found in a distant and separate *power over* something or someone, but rather in the intimate experience of being wounded *for* and *with*.

This contemplative vision of God as vulnerable, woundable, brings about a fresh sense of intercessory prayer as well. Though we often think of intercessory prayer as praying *to* God for the sake of someone else, the contemplatives often sense an invitation to pray *with* God, to share God's joy and sorrow, which in turn God is sharing with all creation. There is a notion here of "keeping God company" in whatever God is experiencing. If John and Teresa are correct that in moments of realized union a person's will and desire are indistinguishable from God's, then there is a role for human beings to play in sharing, if only in microscopic ways, all of God's experience. With the unbelievable intimacy the contemplatives claim we have with God, how could it be any other way?

In truth, I have to say the idea that my own joys and sufferings might in some way be a sharing of God's joy and suffering is even more gratifying and reassuring to me than trusting that God is present with me in my own life experience. If I don't try to comprehend the vast meaning of keeping God company, I like the idea very much indeed.

I want to close with the beginning stanzas of Teresa's poem *"Buscando a Dios,"* "Seeking God." She wrote these verses in response to words she heard in prayer.

Alma, buscarte has en Mi	Soul, you must seek yourself in Me
Y a Mi buscarme has en ti.	And in yourself seek Me.
De tal suerte pudo amor,	With such skill, soul
Alma, en mi te retratar,	Love could portray you in Me
Que ningún sabio pintor	That a painter well gifted
Supiera con tal primor	Could never show
Tal imagen estampar.	So finely that image.
Fuiste por amor criada	For love you were fashioned
Hermosa, bella, y asi	Deep within me
En mis entrañas pintada,	Painted so beautiful, so fair;
Si te perdieres, mi amada,	If, my beloved, you are lost,
Alma, buscarte has en Mi.	Soul, seek yourself in Me.[9]

NOTES

Introduction

1. Harold Kushner, *When Bad Things Happen to Good People* (New York: Schocken Books, 1981), pp. 142–43.
2. Dag Hammarskjöld, *Markings* (New York: Knopf, 1966), p. 205. Hammarskjöld wrote these words in 1961, a few months before he died.
3. *Noche oscura, The Dark Night*, st. 5.
4. *Life*, chaps. 13, 18.
5. Kushner, *When Bad Things Happen to Good People*, p. 147.

Chapter One

1. James Carroll, *Constantine's Sword* (New York: Houghton Mifflin, 2001), pp. 323–24.
2. The mysterious "St. Dionysius" whom John quoted (*The Ascent of Mount Carmel*, bk. 2, chap. 8), now generally called Pseudo-Dionysius, is considered to have lived in the sixth century. His writings were well known to John and his contemporaries, who believed him to be the Dionysius whose conversion by Paul is described in Acts 17:34. In England two centuries before John, the anonymous author of *The Cloud of Unknowing* and the Augustinian monk Walter Hilton had used "darkness" in a manner similar to John's and also made reference to Dionysius.
It is remotely possible that John may have read some of their works that had been translated into Latin, but he never mentioned them. See, for example, Walter Hilton's use of the term "spiritual night" in his *Ladder of Perfection*, pt. 2, chap. 5. For a

commentary on similarities between John of the Cross's work and that of the author of *The Cloud of Unknowing*, see William Johnston's translation of the latter work (New York: Doubleday, 1973), pp. 30–31.

3. *Life*, chap. 1.
4. *Life*, chaps. 25, 29.
5. *Life*, chaps. 24, 25.
6. *Life*, chap. 30.
7. *Life*, chap. 25.
8. This short poem was found in Teresa's breviary after her death. Her longtime friend, Fr. Jerónimo Gracián, authenticated it. It is generally known by its first line, although it is sometimes called "Teresa's Bookmark."
9. The "hallmarks" I note here are not the classical signs of the dark night delineated by John. I will describe those later.
10. For a succinct history of the Carmelite order and tradition, see John Welch, *The Carmelite Tradition*, available online at www.carmelite.org/tradition.htm.
11. *Life*, chap. 32.
12. *Life*, chap. 36. ˙
13. *Foundations*, chap. 1.
14. *Foundations*, chap. 2.
15. At the time, the Carthusians were noted for their very austere lifestyle. Some two centuries later, in order to relieve their impoverishment, they began to market an "elixir of long life" made from a secret recipe. This was to become the famous Chartreuse liqueur, which continues to be distilled by the Carthusian monks today.
16. Concerning *"mi Senequita"* and *"santico,"* see E. A. Peers, trans., *The Letters of Saint Teresa of Jesus* (Westminster, MD: Newman, 1950), vol. 1, p. 13. For "a friar and a half," see E. A. Peers, *Spirit of Flame* (London: Sheed and Ward, 1943), pp. 18–19. Although it is generally assumed Teresa was making a joke about John's height, it is possible—though unlikely—that by the "half" she might have meant Fray Antonio, about whom she had some lingering reservations.
17. *Foundations*, chap. 3; a 1568 letter to Don Francisco de Salcedo, in Peers, trans., *Letters of Saint Teresa*, vol. 1, p. 52.

18. From one of her "minor works," *Vejamen sobre las palabras "Búscate en Mí,"* "Judgment on the Words 'Seek Yourself in Me.'" Translations of this delightful piece of Teresa's humor can be found in K. Kavanaugh and O. Rodriguez, trans., *The Collected Works of St. Teresa of Ávila* (Washington, DC: Institute of Carmelite Studies, 1985), vol. 3, pp. 357–62, and in E. A. Peers, trans., *Complete Works of St. Teresa* (London: Sheed and Ward, 1975), pp. 215–18, 266–68. The passage continues, "Nevertheless, we are grateful for his having given us such a good explanation of what we had not asked about."

19. Peers, trans., *Letters of Saint Teresa*, vol. 1, pp. 482–84, 488. The companion abducted with John was Father Germán de San Matias.

20. Peers, trans., *Letters of Saint Teresa*, vol. 1, pp. 495–98.

21. K. Kavanaugh and O. Rodriguez, trans., *The Collected Works of St. John of the Cross* (Washington, DC: Institute of Carmelite Studies, 1991), p. 19.

22. John terms it *"luz en general,"* literally "light in general," and says, "for it would be ignorant to think that what love says through mystical knowing, as in these stanzas, could be explained by any kind of words" (prologue to the commentary on *The Spiritual Canticle*). In this context, John also frequently quotes St. Paul's words about the Spirit praying in "sighs too deep for words" (Rom. 8:26).

23. *The Way of Perfection,* chap. 17. Note John's even more powerful statement in the commentary on st. 3 of *The Living Flame of Love* (first redaction): "God leads souls along such different paths that it is unlikely to find one spirit who can walk even halfway along the path of another."

24. *Living Flame,* commentary on st. 1. It should be noted that John's wording cannot legitimately be interpreted as saying that human beings *are* God. In *The Ascent of Mount Carmel* (bk. 2, chap. 5), for example, John says, "No creature, nor any actions or abilities, can encompass or attain that which is God." Further, in his commentary on *The Living Flame,* John speaks of the soul as having deeper and deeper "centers" in God and, never satisfied, always going deeper throughout life.

Notes

Chapter Two

1. Alice Walker, *The Color Purple* (New York: Washington Square, 1982), p. 177.
2. This understanding is identical to the biblical use of the Hebrew term *nephesh*, "soul": the essence of a person. To be precise, John does not *equate* the soul with the physical body, and in fact acknowledges that the soul "is a spirit," *"el alma, en cuanto espíritu"* (*The Living Flame of Love*, commentary on st. 1). Again, though, this is not a matter of seeing separate parts of people, but rather of seeing people spiritually.
3. From her poem *"Buscando a Dios,"* "Seeking God." (Also see Chapter 1, n. 18 above.)
4. St. Augustine, *Confessions*, bk. 3, chap. 6; John, *Living Flame*, commentary on st. 1: "[Through this union, God] . . . preserves [creatures'] being; if this were to fail, they would instantly be annihilated and cease to exist."
5. *"Para entender, pues, cuál sea esta unión de que vamos tratando, es de saber que Dios, en cualquiera alma, aunque sea la del mayor pecador del mundo, mora y asiste sustancialmente. Y esta manera de unión siempre está hecha entre Dios y las criaturas todas"* (*The Ascent of Mount Carmel*, bk. 2, chap. 5).
6. *The Interior Castle*, First Mansions, chap. 1.
7. *Noetic Sciences Review* 40 (winter 1996): 32. Discussed more fully in Parker J. Palmer, *Let Your Life Speak* (San Francisco: Jossey-Bass, 2000).
8. A nationwide poll indicated that 82 percent of Americans believe that the "God helps those who help themselves" saying comes from the Bible. In truth it began in ancient Greece and was popularized in more modern times by Benjamin Franklin, who recorded it in his *Poor Richard's Almanack*. Adolf Hitler also used the saying to stir up Nazi spirit in the 1930s. The Bible, of course, says nothing of the sort. If anything, it maintains the opposite: that God helps those who *cannot* help themselves. Similarly, the saying about prayer is often attributed to St. Ignatius of Loyola. But he too said essentially the opposite: pray as if everything depends upon yourself; act as if everything depends upon God. For an article on these sayings, see my "Propaganda of Willfulness," in *Shalem News* 25, no. 1 (winter 2001), available online at www.shalem.org/sn/25.1ggm.html.

9. *"... para llegar a la divina luz de la unión perfecta del amor de Dios"* (*Ascent*, prologue). Italics mine.
10. *Living Flame*, commentary on st. 1.
11. St. Augustine, *Confessions*, bk. 1, chap. 1.
12. *Soliloquies*, *(Exclamaciones)* no. 3.
13. *Living Flame*, st. 4, poem and commentary.
14. Teresa describes the inhabitants of the castle in *Interior Castle*, First Mansions, chap. 2. The Institute of Carmelite Studies translation has Teresa saying of the faculties, "What bad management!" K. Kavanaugh and O. Rodriguez, trans., *The Collected Works of St. Teresa of Ávila* (Washington, DC: Institute of Carmelite Studies, 1980), vol. 2, p. 289.
15. I am indebted to Fr. John Welch, O.Carm., for laying out the basics of this diagram for me. See his description in John Welch, *When Gods Die* (New York: Paulist, 1990), pp. 55ff.
16. *Sayings of Light and Love*, 60.
17. *Living Flame*, commentary on st. 2.
18. *Ascent*, bk. 2, chap. 26.
19. In truth, what is said here about the essence of God could be said about anyone or anything—even ourselves. We can know certain things *about* something or someone and have images and concepts *of* them, but their true essence remains forever somehow beyond our grasp.
20. There are many reproductions of John's sketch of the mountain. A nice side-by-side Spanish-English version is in K. Kavanaugh and O. Rodriguez, trans., *The Collected Works of St. John of the Cross* (Washington, DC: Institute of Carmelite Studies, 1991), pp. 110–11.
21. *The Spiritual Canticle*, st. 1. For "God's games," see *Living Flame*, commentary on st. 1. Teresa refers to *"esta guerra de amor,"* "this war of love," in her collection known as *Soliloquies*, *(Exclamaciones)*, or *Cries of the Soul to God*, no. 16, entitled "The Wounds of Love."
22. See John, *Spiritual Canticle*, st. 6: "Send me no more messengers." Also see Teresa, *Life*, chap. 14: "God is so near [the soul] that it need not send Him messengers, but can speak with Him directly."
23. I have described at length the psychology and neurology of attachment and addiction in *Addiction and Grace* (San Francisco: HarperSanFrancisco, 1991).

Notes

Chapter Three

1. L. Barkway and L. Menzies, eds., *An Anthology of the Love of God: From the Writings of Evelyn Underhill* (Wilton, CT: Morehouse-Barlow, 1976), p. 100.
2. Brother Lawrence, *The Practice of the Presence of God*, trans. Sr. Mary David (New York: Paulist, 1978), p. 89.
3. *"Son tan oscuras de entender estas cosas interiores"* and *". . . al demonio, que como es las mismas tinieblas"* (*The Interior Castle*, First Mansions, chap. 2, pars. 7, 1).
4. *The Living Flame of Love*, commentary on st. 3.
5. *Maxims on Love*, 54; *The Dark Night*, st. 5.
6. *The Ascent of Mount Carmel*, bk. 1, chap. 14.
7. John, *Dark Night*, bk. 1, chap. 14. Teresa's speaking of Christ's surrender *to* us has a unique flavor, since most Christian writings speak of God's surrendering Christ *for* us, for our sins. Yet Teresa is clearly talking about Christ giving himself *to* us. For example: *"con tanto amor se nos dio,"* "surrendered [gave] himself to us with such fullness of love" (*The Way of Perfection*, chap. 33, first redaction).
8. For example: *"dos maneras: la una es activa; la otra, pasiva,"* "two manners: the one is active; the other, passive" (*Ascent*, bk. 1, chap. 13).
9. Apparently, the person responsible for first floating the idea of acquired contemplation was the sixteenth-century Spanish Carmelite Tomás de Jesus, who not only compiled John's works but also inserted some of his own writings, which were later taken to be John's. For an excellent and scholarly look at these distortions, including their impact on today's understanding of spirituality, see James Arraj, *From St. John of the Cross to Us: The Story of a 400 Year Long Misunderstanding and What It Means for the Future of Christian Mysticism* (Chiloquin, OR: Inner Growth Books, 1999). Information and current dialogue about this work is also available online at www.innerexplorations.com.
10. *Living Flame*, commentary on st. 3.
11. *Living Flame*, commentary on st. 3 (second redaction).
12. *Living Flame*, commentary on st. 3 (second redaction).
13. *Dark Night*, bk. 1, chap. 8.
14. *Ascent*, bk. 2, chap. 3.

15. *Ascent,* bk. 2, chaps. 6–12.
16. *Ascent,* bk. 2, chap. 5.
17. *Ascent,* bk. 1, chap. 13.
18. *Ascent,* bk. 1, chap. 14.
19. *"No hay estado de oración tan subido, que muchas veces no sea necesario tornar al principio,"* "There is no state of prayer so high that it would not often be necessary to return to the beginning" (*Life,* chap. 13).
20. *Dark Night,* bk. 2, chap. 5.
21. Constance FitzGerald, "Transformation in Wisdom," in K. Culligan and R. Jordan, eds., *Carmelite Studies VIII: Carmel and Contemplation* (Washington, DC: Institute of Carmelite Studies, 2000), pp. 309–10.
22. *Living Flame,* poem and commentary, sts. 1, 4.
23. *". . . con grande conformidad de las partes, donde lo que tú quieres que pida, pido, y lo que no quieres, no quiero ni aun puedo ni me pasa por pensamiento querer"* (*Living Flame,* st. 1, par. 36).
24. Bernard of Clairvaux (1090–1153), *Treatise on the Love of God* or *On Loving God,* chaps. 8–10.
25. Teresa, *Interior Castle,* First Mansions, chap. 1; John, *Living Flame,* commentary on st. 4.

Chapter Four

1. James Montgomery (1771–1854), English journalist and poet. Written in 1818 for Edward Bickersteth's *Treatise on Prayer,* this poem later became the first stanza of the hymn "Prayer Is the Soul's Sincere Desire," in Montgomery's own words, "the most attractive hymn I ever wrote."
2. *The Way of Perfection,* chap. 25.
3. *The Interior Castle,* Fourth Mansions, chap. 3; Sixth Mansions, chap. 7; *The Way of Perfection,* chap. 29.
4. *Interior Castle,* Fourth Mansions, chap. 3.
5. *The Ascent of Mount Carmel,* bk. 2, chap. 13.
6. See Chapter 3, n. 9.
7. Hugh of St. Victor, *Selected Spiritual Writings* (New York: Harper & Row, 1962), p. 183; Teresa, *Interior Castle,* Sixth Mansions, chap. 8: *". . . hace advertir a todo la presencia que trae cabe sí."*

8. "Continuously renewed immediacy, not receding memory of the Divine Touch, lies at the base of religious living." Thomas Kelly, *A Testament of Devotion* (New York: Harper & Brothers, 1941), p. 31.
9. Kelly, *Testament*, p. 95.
10. Teresa, *Life*, chap. 29; John, *Ascent*, bk. 2, chap. 24.
11. For a comprehensive listing of classical quotations describing contemplation, see www.shalem.org/quotes.html.
12. Teresa's discussion of the interior garden is in her *Life*, chaps. 11–22. She added these chapters some two years after completing the original text. Unless otherwise indicated, quotations cited about the garden come from these chapters.
13. *Life*, chaps. 9, 12, 13; *Way of Perfection*, chaps. 26, 28, 29; Letter 122 to Gracián: "The most potent and acceptable prayer is the prayer that leaves the best effects."
14. *Life*, chap. 11. She continues: "Without that [the help of God], as we know, we cannot think a single good thought."
15. *Interior Castle*, Fourth Mansions, chap. 1–3.
16. *Life*, chap. 14.
17. *Interior Castle*, Fourth Mansions, chap. 1. Teresa sensed this distinction early on, as she wrote her *Life*, but it was not until the *Interior Castle* that she described it clearly.
18. *Life*, chaps. 14–15.
19. *Life*, chaps. 11, 14.
20. *Interior Castle*, Fourth Mansions, chaps. 2–3; *Life*, chap. 7.
21. *Interior Castle*, Fourth Mansions, chaps. 1–2; *Life*, chap. 7.
22. *Life*, chaps. 15, 17.
23. *Life*, chaps. 16–17.
24. Examples of texts with which Teresa was familiar include Francisco de Osuna's *Third Spiritual Alphabet*, Bernardino de Laredo's *The Ascent of Mount Sion*, and Jerome's *Letters*.
25. *Life*, chaps. 15–17.
26. *Life*, chaps. 16–17.
27. *Life*, chap. 18.
28. This "understanding by not understanding" is a classical theme in Christian contemplative tradition. The third-century theologian Origen, sometimes called the father of Christian mysticism, used the Greek word *mystikos* not to describe something unexplained, but as a *way of knowing*. Pseudo-Dionysius, who had

such a powerful influence on the mystical theology of John and Teresa, also saw unknowing as a particularly profound way of knowing.

29. *Life,* chap. 18.

Chapter Five

1. Oscar Wilde, *Lady Windermere's Fan* (1892), act 1.
2. *The Dark Night,* bk. 1, chap. 9.
3. *The Living Flame of Love,* commentary on st. 3.
4. *Dark Night,* bk. 1, chap. 9; *The Ascent of Mount Carmel,* bk. 2, chaps. 13–14; *Living Flame,* commentary on st. 3.
5. *Ascent,* bk. 2, chap. 12.
6. *Dark Night,* bk. 1, chap. 9.
7. This is a combination of what John describes as the first sign in the *Ascent,* bk. 2, chap. 13, and the first and third signs in the *Dark Night,* bk. 1, chap. 9.
8. This is a combination of the second signs John describes in both the *Ascent* and the *Dark Night.* The quotations are from *Dark Night,* bk. 1, chap. 9. I will say more about the dark night and depression in the next chapter.
9. This is the third "and surest" sign John lists in the *Ascent,* bk. 2, chap. 13, from which the quotations are taken. John also mentions it in his discussion of the second sign in *Dark Night,* bk. 1, chap. 9.
10. John's description of these spirits is in *Dark Night,* bk. 1, chap. 14. He associates them primarily with the dark night of the senses. Unless otherwise indicated, all quotations are taken from that source.
11. The early church father Tertullian, for example, said: "He who serves false gods is doubtless an adulterer of truth, because all falsehood is adultery. So, too, he is sunk in fornication. For who that is a fellow-worker with unclean spirits, does not stalk in general pollution and fornication? And thus it is that the Holy Scriptures use the designation of fornication in their upbraiding of idolatry" (*On Idolatry,* chap. 1, probably written in the very early third century).
12. *The Spiritual Canticle,* st. 1. From *The Collected Works of St. John of the Cross,* translated by Kieran Kavanaugh and Otilio Rodriguez, copyright © 1964, 1979, 1991 by Washington Province of

Discalced Carmelites ICS Publications, 2131 Lincoln Road N.E., Washington, DC 20012–1199, U.S.A., www.icspublications.org (1991), p. 44. Reprinted by permission.

13. Teresa, *"Ayes del destierro,"* "Sighs in Exile," st. 8.
14. This may be the most famous quote attributed to Teresa and it is certainly in keeping with her personality, but I have never been able to verify it in her writings or in any other reliable source.
15. For a detailed description of the neurological and spiritual dynamics of habituation, tolerance, and other aspects of this process, see my *Addiction and Grace* (San Francisco: HarperSanFrancisco, 1991).

Chapter Six

1. Walt Whitman, "Years of the Modern," in *Selections from Leaves of Grass* (New York: Crown, 1961), p. 100.
2. The sources for Teresa's and John's insights on melancholia and other mental illnesses are too numerous to list completely. As examples, however, see Teresa, *The Interior Castle*, Sixth Mansions, chaps. 1–3, and especially her *Foundations*, chap. 7. See also John, *The Dark Night*, bk. 1, chaps. 4, 9.
3. Gerald May, *Care of Mind, Care of Spirit* (San Francisco: Harper & Row, 1982), pp. 84–92.
4. *Dark Night*, bk. 1, chap. 9.
5. This is a very brief selection from the National Institute of Mental Health pamphlet entitled *Depression* (Bethesda, MD: NIMH Publication No. 00–3561, 2000), available from NIMH Public Inquiries, 6001 Executive Boulevard, Rm. 8184, MSC 9663, Bethesda, MD 20892–9663; (301) 443–4513; fax (301) 443–4279; www.nimh.nih.gov/publicat/depression.cfm#ptdep3.
6. *Dark Night*, bk. 1, chap. 9.
7. Judith Hooper, "Prozac and Enlightened Mind," *Tricycle: The Buddhist Review* (summer 1999): 38–110.
8. See my *Addiction and Grace* (San Francisco: HarperSanFrancisco, 1991) for more details. A more recent review article with references to specific studies is Eric Nestler, "Molecular Basis of Long-Term Plasticity Underlying Addiction," *Nature Reviews* 2 (February 2001).

9. I described these dynamics also in my "Lightness of Soul: From Addiction Toward Love in John of the Cross," *Spiritual Life* (fall 1991).
10. John, *The Living Flame of Love*, commentary on st. 3; Teresa, *Life*, chap. 13. These two sources contain a wealth of recommendations about spiritual direction.
11. *Living Flame*, commentary on st. 3.
12. *Living Flame*, commentary on st. 3.
13. *Living Flame*, commentary on st. 3. All the following quotations come from this source unless otherwise specified.
14. *Foundations*, chap. 21.
15. His Holiness the Fourteenth Dalai Lama, Tenzin Gyatso, in Thich Nhat Hanh, *Peace Is Every Step* (New York: Bantam, 1991), p. vii.
16. First proposed by Ludwig von Bertalanffy in the 1940s, systems theory can apply to any collection of entities: from molecules, cells, and organs to species, environments, and the social systems mentioned here.

Chapter Seven
1. Irenaeus, Bishop of Lyons (second century C.E.), *Against Heresies* 4.20.7.
2. *The Spiritual Canticle*, commentary on sts. 14–15.
3. *The Living Flame of Love*, st. 4, from *The Collected Works of St. John of the Cross*, translated by Kieran Kavanaugh and Otilio Rodriguez, copyright © 1964, 1979, 1991 by Washington Province of Discalced Carmelites ICS Publications, 2131 Lincoln Road N.E., Washington, DC 20012–1199, U.S.A., www.icspublications.org (1991), p. 53. Reprinted with permission.
4. *Living Flame*, commentary on st. 4.
5. *The Interior Castle*, Seventh Mansions, chaps. 1–2.
6. *The Dark Night*, bk. 2, chap. 1. Not only is John speaking of the dark night of the senses here, but he also appears to be referring to people who are not destined for "so high a degree of love" as some others might be. Still, he is clearly describing the existence of periodic, intermittent experiences of the dawn and would be loath to predict what God has in mind for any person.

7. John, *Living Flame*, commentary on sts. 1, 3; *Spiritual Canticle*, commentary on st. 26; Teresa, *Interior Castle*, Fifth Mansions, chap. 2; Seventh Mansions, chap. 3.
8. Ps. 102:7, Modern King James Version; Teresa, *Life*, chap. 20; John, *Spiritual Canticle*, commentary on st. 15.
9. Teresa, "Seeking God," from *The Collected Works of St. Teresa of Ávila*, vol. 3, translated by Kieran Kavanaugh and Otilio Rodriguez, copyright © 1980 by Washington Province of Discalced Carmelites ICS Publications, 2131 Lincoln Road N.E., Washington, DC 20012–1199, U.S.A., www.icspublications.org (1985), p. 385. Reprinted by permission. Note: I have corrected what I believe are translation errors in the last two lines.

INDEX

213

Index

Index